What I Can Be
When I Grow Up

Permission to Dream

What I Can Be
When I Grow Up

Permission to Dream

Written by Ophelia S. Lewis
Illustrated by Shabamukama Osbert

VILLAGE TALES PUBLISHING

MINNEAPOLIS, MN

What I Can Be When I Grow Up

Copyright © 2022 by Ophelia S. Lewis

Cover & Design by: OASS

ISBN-13: 978-1-945408-16-8

ISBN-10: 1945408162

Library of Congress Control Number: 2022906909

Village Tales Publishing
www.villagetalespublishing.com
Email: villagetalespub@gmail.com

Give feedback on the book at:
villagetalespub@gmail.com

Printed in U.S.A.

Dedication

To my precious grandchildren;
Elijah, Logan, London, Lydia, Ian, and Liyah.
and
To all the children of Liberia, Africa, and the world.
Being educated will be the most important aspect of your career
path. **Learn as much as you can to be able to give to others**.
When we care for one another, we make the world a safer and
more peaceful place to live. Prepare and be excited about your
future and your life.

"Without Reading and Writing, a person is blind,
a nation is doom, and the world is lost."
- Mac N. Nelson, Liberian author (Bottom Up)

"Girls with dreams become women with visions."
- Meghan Markle, (Prince Harry's wife)

"If you have a positive frame of mind,
you can manifest positive things in your life."
- Alesha Dixon, (British musician)

"I've always believed that if you put in the work,
the results will come."
- Michael Jordan, (won NBA championships
six times with the Chicago Bulls)

Contents

What am I Missing?

Introduction

A community is a group of people living in a particular area, whether a neighborhood, a village, a town, a small or big city, or even a global community (the world). We all live together in a community. We depend on one another for various necessities of life, like food, clothing, or shelter.

A community helper is anyone that helps keep our community functioning well. Naturally, this would include police, firefighters, doctors, and garbage collectors. But it also includes market women, street vendors, nurses, chefs, bakers, astronauts, soldiers, teachers, dentists, mail carriers, bus and taxi drivers, coaches, babysitters, fishermen, plumbers, farmers, librarians, and volunteers.

What will happen without community helpers? We cannot even imagine a day without the help of community helpers. Our necessities will stop if we get no service or help from doctors, nurses, market women, bankers, soldiers, teachers, taxi drivers, dentists, etc. Therefore, every community helper is essential and must get our support and respect for their helpful services. When we care for one another, we make the world a safer and more peaceful place.

Communities help individuals solve problems, stay motivated and overcome obstacles. When you grow up, you will be part of the community helpers. People in the community matter to one another. Their needs will be met through commitment and togetherness. Being a part of a community can make us feel like we are a part of something greater than ourselves. Community means participation. Community means giving back.

So, what does community mean to you? What community helper are you inspired to be? I hope this book helps you know what it will take to be what you want to be when you grow up; a productive community helper.

"Alone, we can do so little;
together, we can do so much."
– Helen Keller

Inspired to Be What I Can Be

Do you like to go to school?

Do you like to study?

Do you make good grades?

Do you like science?

Do you like animals?

Do you like math or history?

Do you like to know how things work?

Do you have a clever way of doing things?

Do you like to draw?

Do you like to tell strories or make up your own story?

Do you like to sing or dance?

What are your talents?

What community helper would you like to be?

Be inspired by the success of others.

Talent and Effort

Everyone has one or more talents. Talents are special abilities. We're all talented in different ways and those talents come from God. Someone might be good at singing, drawing or playing sports and that's a special gift or talent they got from God. He wants us to discover our talents and develop them. When we practice and work hard to understand our talents, then we will be able to use them to help in our community.

Identifying and sharing your talents

Sometimes people think they have no talents, but that is only because they don't see the things they do as talents. Our talents of many shapes and sizes can help everyone in the community. We can share with others the talents (gifts) we enjoy: gifts of art, of music and science, of carpentry and farming and nursing, gifts of engineering and housekeeping, of law, of teaching, gifts of caring for children and of tending to the old and the ill, and philanthropy. Philanthropy is the giving and sharing of time, talent or wealth intended for the common good (use by everyone).

Are you really good at helping people when they are sad or mad? Do you have the patience to listen? Do you know just what to say to help them feel better? How can you help others with these talents in the community?

I am good at putting things in order.
I am a good leader.
I am good at improving things.
I am good at making lists.
I am ood at caring for others.
I am good at working in groups.
I am good at sorting into groups.
I am good at fixing things.
I am a good mediator.
I am good at finding answers.
I am good at planning.
I am good at finding things out.
I am good at helping others.
I am good with my hands.
I am good at drawing.
I am good at building teams.
I am a good speaker.
I am good with numbers.
I am good at thinking creatively.

A FEW TALENTS YOU MIGHT HAVE

I am good at knowing what to do.
I am good at writing.
I pay attention to detail.
I am a good listener.
I am reliable.
I am organised.
I work well with others.
I am good at making decisions.
I am good at solving problems.
I am good with other people.
I am a good manager.

Being Successful

Many of us want to be successful people. What does it mean to be successful? A successful person is someone who reaches their dreams or goal, or does something important. Two things that help someone be successful are talent and effort.

TALENT + EFFORT

Natural talent is something you're good at that comes very easy to you. Someone who is naturally talented at sports might be able to beat someone at basketball without even practicing, even though the other person did practice. Someone who is naturally talented at math might understand a concept much more quickly than someone else without having to try very hard.

Effort is how hard you work and how much you push yourself. If you're not naturally talented at something, you'll have to put in more effort and work harder to achieve what you want. What do you think matters more in becoming a successful person?

Natural talent ISN'T the most important thing to being successful. To be successful, effort matters A LOT more than natural talent. Many people think that natural talent matters more and that to be successful, things should come easily to them. Actually, effort usually matters a lot more. However, effort and hard work can also make you become even better at things that do come naturally to you.

PERSEVERE

Persevere means to keep trying to do something even though it is difficult. Learned how to persevere, so when things become hard, you never give up or switched to something easier. Natural talent and effort are both good things. It's important to make sure you challenge yourself to do hard things instead of only sticking with things you're naturally good at.

Use Your Brain.

Meet Your Brain

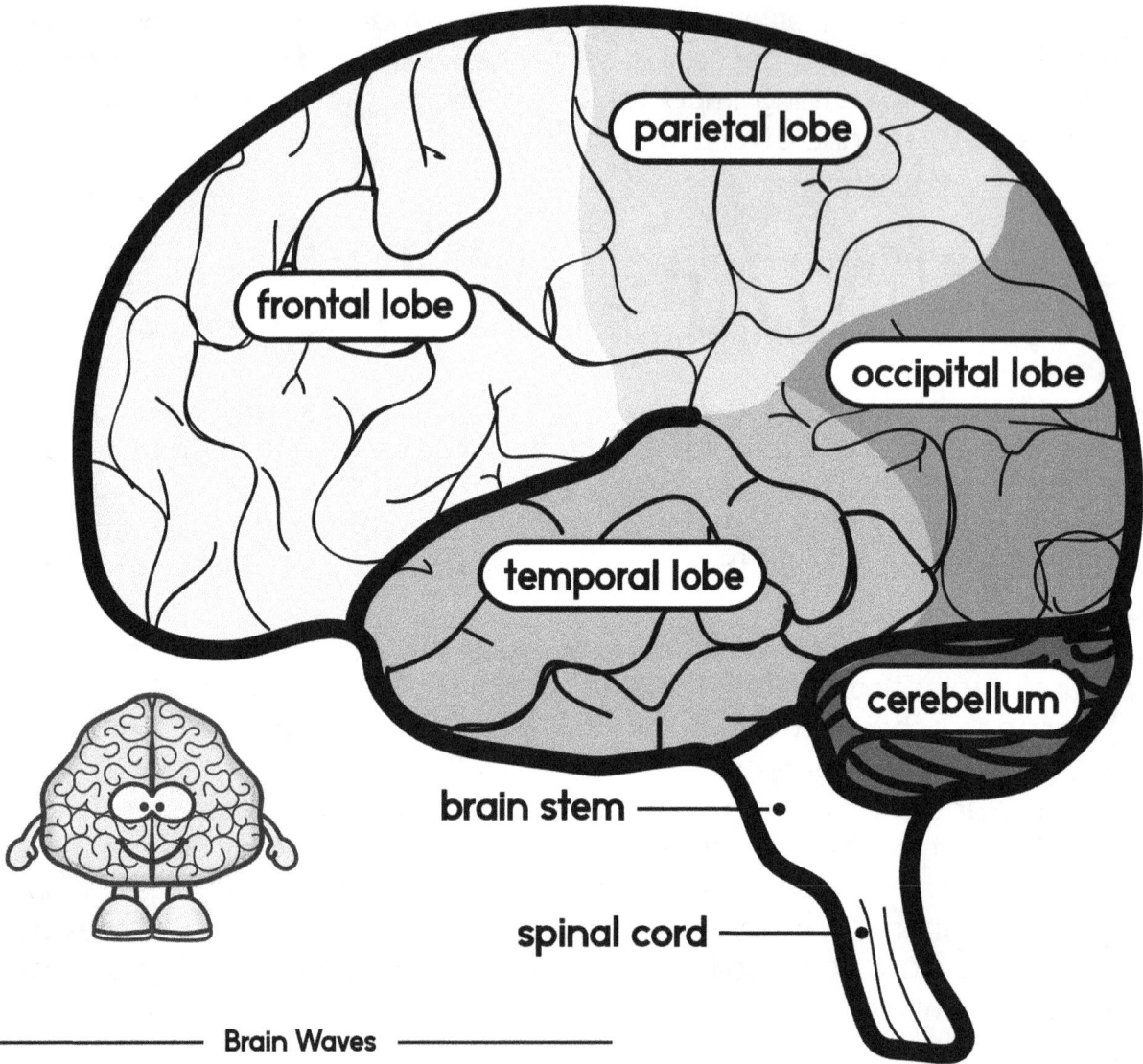

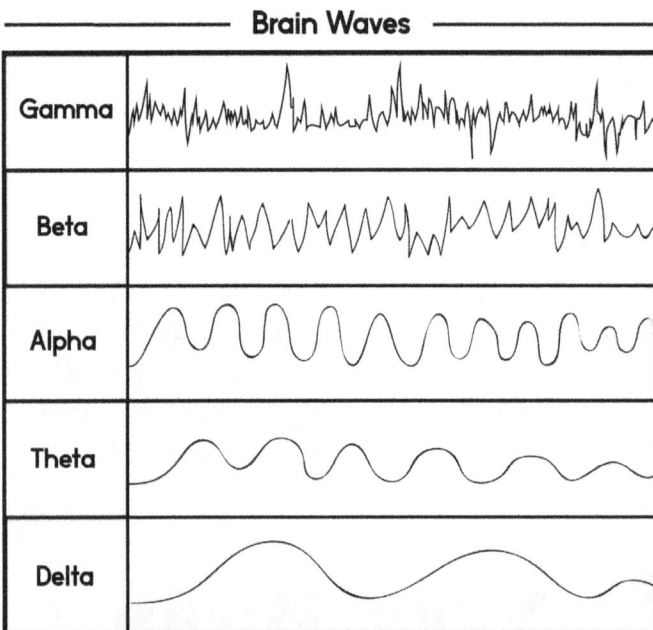

parietal lobe

frontal lobe

occipital lobe

temporal lobe

cerebellum

brain stem

spinal cord

Brain Waves

Gamma	
Beta	
Alpha	
Theta	
Delta	

Frontal lobe - Decision making takes place here. The frontal lobe is in charge of thinking, reasoning, decision-making, and planning for the future. Our personality is also housed in the frontal lobe!

The parietal lobe manages taste, hearing, sight, touch, and smell. For example, our parietal lobe helps our brain understand whether we are standing up, lying down, or hanging upside-down on the monkey bars!

The temporal lobe is in charge of

many things, including hearing, language, and memory! The temporal lobe is in charge of a particular part of memory that allows us to remember words, objects, faces, and more!

The occipital lobe is located right at the back of the brain, and it has an essential job. The occipital lobe houses our visual cortex, so it helps us see. The occipital lobe receives information from millions of cells in our eyes and processes all of that information to help us understand what we are seeing. The cells in our eyes collect information about light, and then our occipital lobe has to turn that information into a picture with color, texture, size, distance, and much more. Since we have two eyes, our occipital lobe also has to combine information from both eyes so that we only see one picture.

The cerebellum is at the back of the brain, below the cerebrum. It's a lot smaller than the cerebrum. But it's an essential part of the brain. It controls balance, movement, and coordination (how your muscles work together). Cerebellum - controls our muscles.

Other parts of the brain not shown in the diagram on page 14.

The amygdala is a small almond shaped structure located deep in the brain. The amygdala is responsible for processing and expressing emotions; strong feelins like anger, love, joy, or fear. When the amygdala senses danger, it can overrule parts of the brain and take over, enabling us to act before we think, a highly useful survival response.

The cerebrum is the largest part of the brain. It is in the front part of the brain. It contains about 15 billion cells, and is the latest brain structure to have evolved. The cerebrum takes in data from sight and other sense organs, and 'makes sense' of it (interprets it). It controls consciousness and action (voluntary muscular activity). It plans, thinks, judges, and organises speech and information. Cerebrum - thinking, memories, and solving problems.

The hippocampus is a special structure found deep within the brain. It has a very important job involving memories. It is possible to recall both old and new memories because of Hippocampus - that's where our long term memory is.

Another brain part that's small but mighty is the brain stem. The brain stem sits beneath the cerebrum and in front of the cerebellum. It connects the rest of the brain to the spinal cord, which runs down your neck and back. The brain stem is in charge of all the functions your body needs to stay alive, like breathing air, digesting food, and circulating blood.

The Brain is Like a Muscle

Your brain gets stronger
when you learn
something new.

Your brain gets stronger
when you gladly
accept a challenge.

Mindset

We use our brain to think. Mindset is a way of thinking. It is the way our brain sees ourselves and the world. Our mindset helps us look at problems and mistakes in a positive way. Our thought habits affect how we think, what we feel, and what we do. Our mindset influences how we make sense of the world, and how we make sense of our self.

Smart is something you become, NOT something you are.

Growth Mindset

A person's abilities and intelligence can be developed through practice, hard work, dedication, and motivation.

A growth mindset is believing in the power of yourself and your brain. A growth mindset is when we know, and with practice, we will get better at something. Having a growth mindset means . . . I know my brain can change, grow, and learn!

I have a growth mindset!

I like to challenge myself.

I will practice to improve.

I will work hard to make progress.

I am inspired by people who succeed.

My effort and attitude make all the difference. I will keep a great attitude.

I will keep trying, even when it gets hard.

Mistakes help me learn. I will stick with it until I get it.

I can learn anything that I want to.

Education is important!

Growth Mindset vs Fixed Mindset

Growth mindset is a concept developed by Carol Dweck, a Professor of Psychology at Stanford University. It is believed that a person's abilities and intelligence can be acquired through practice, hard work, dedication, and motivation.

A fixed mindset is a notion that intelligence and talent alone will lead to success. People with a fixed mindset believe that these things are "fixed" and cannot be developed or improved. They think you are either born with it or not, and nothing can change that.

Growth mindset is the idea that everyone has the ability to develop in their intelligence and talent.

Fixed mindset is the idea that your intelligence and talent cannot be improved. You were either born with it or not. Nothing can change it.

"If I practice every night for 20 minutes, I will learn my multiplication."

"I'm not good at math, so I will never learn my math."

HOW TO ENCOURAGE A GROWTH MINDSET IN YOURSELF AND OTHERS.

Take on challenges.

Give 100% effort.

Seek feedback from others.

Don't get discouraged by mistakes.

Use problem-solving strategies.

Set goals for yourself.

Ask questions when you don't understand.

Actively solve problems instead of reacting to them.

Monitor your progress so you can see your growth.

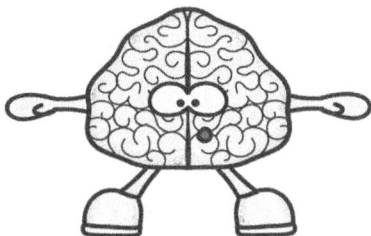

Always wear your thinking cap.

Change Your Mindset

Find the hidden words in the puzzle. Remember, words run not only vertically, horizontally, and diagonally but may also be spelled backward. If you get stuck, the answers are included at the back of the book.

GROWTH
CHALLENGE
POSITIVE
PROBLEM SOLVER
ATTITUDE
INTELLIGENCE
EFFORT
OPTIMISM
SUCCESS
PROGRESS
HARD WORK
PERSISTENCE
THINK
GOAL SETTING

L	G	N	I	T	T	E	S	L	A	O	G	W	V	R
E	L	P	R	O	B	L	E	M	S	O	L	V	E	R
E	D	L	O	E	C	N	E	T	S	I	S	R	E	P
C	H	U	P	G	T	R	H	L	X	H	N	G	Z	N
N	A	Q	T	G	E	P	O	S	I	T	I	V	E	G
E	R	R	I	I	K	F	L	N	E	W	L	N	R	B
G	D	Q	M	K	T	H	F	G	B	O	P	X	Q	S
I	W	R	I	R	J	T	N	O	R	R	R	M	S	C
L	O	C	S	N	T	E	A	Y	R	G	K	E	S	K
L	R	J	M	L	L	R	X	G	Y	T	R	U	V	J
E	K	K	N	L	L	G	D	D	L	G	C	M	K	M
T	T	V	A	R	P	M	M	T	O	C	J	D	M	X
N	W	H	K	R	K	X	M	R	E	H	P	N	B	L
I	C	K	V	Y	W	R	P	S	M	K	Q	R	Y	C
K	N	I	H	T	C	L	S	Y	K	N	W	D	C	Z

Develop a growth mindset.

1. Mistakes will help me learn new things.
2. Intelligence is not fixed.
3. No giving up!
4. Display a positive attitude.
5. Set goals for myself.
6. Encourage others.
7. Take on challenges.

My brain will do some heavy lifting.

Hopes and Goals

A goal is something that you want to do, to be, or to have, and you don't have the resources [time, money, permission, etc.] to get it right this moment. It is something you will work to get in the future, after you figure out what resources [time, money, permission, etc.] you need in order to get it, achieve it, or do it.

MY EFFORT

AND ATTITUDE

DETERMINE

EVERYTHING.

Setting SMART Goals

S
Specific

M
Measurable

A
Attainable

R
Relevant / Realistic

T
Time-bound Trackable

Specific:
    What exactly is your goal?
    What do you hope to achieve?

Measurable:
    How will you know when you reach your goal?

Attainable:
    What action plan will help you achieve your goal?

Relevant / Realistic:
    Is your goal realistic to your abilities? Does it relate to your interests?

Time-bound / trackable:
    When will you achieve your goal?
    How will you monitor your progress?

Finish the statement below . . .

S
Specific

Specific:
I want to be able to . . .

I want to achieve . . .

M
Measurable

Measurable:
I know I will have met my goal when I . . .

A
Attainable

Attainable:
I know this is an attainable goal because I . . .

R
Relevant
/ Realistic

Relevant / Realistic:
This goal is relevant to me because it builds upon skills I have, like . . .

T
Time-bound
Trackable

Time-bound / Trackable:
I will track this goal each . . .

I will achieve this goal by, . . .

My Hopes and Goals For This School Year

I am in grade: _____

School year: _____

Think about your strengths and areas for improvement. Talk with your teacher/parents about one goal and one hope you have for this school year. Record your ideas below.

One GOAL I have for the school year is . . .

_____

_____

_____

_____

_____

One HOPE I have for the school year is . . .

_____

_____

_____

_____

_____

This is going to take some time.

I can take small towards my goal.

STEPS

Strengths and Weaknesses

my strengths

my areas for improvement

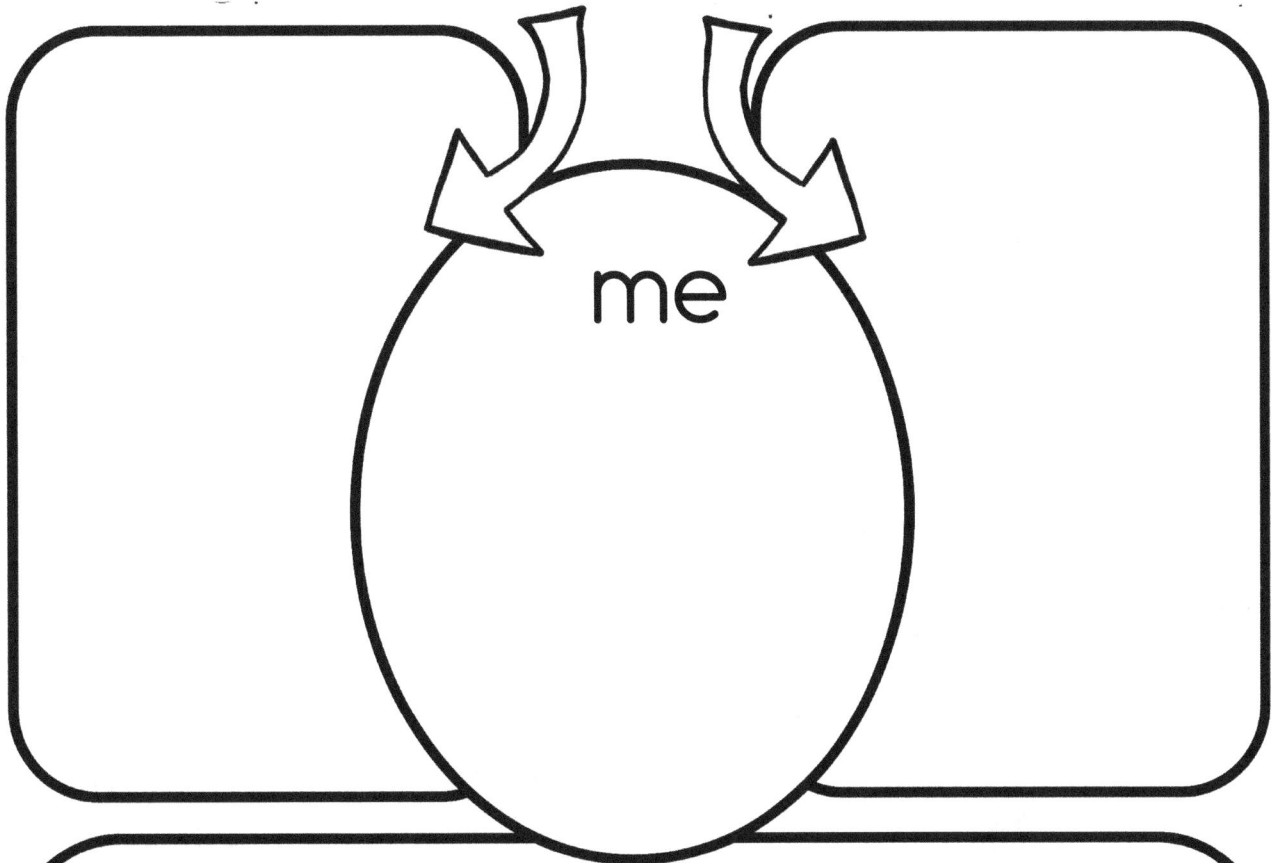

me

I can improve by:

Did you complete your goal?
Don't forget to get your Goal Certificate signed. It's on page 137.

25

What Good is Education?

Education is knowledge, skill, and development gained from study or training. Knowledge means you learn something and keep it in your mind. Education helps you learn. The more you know, the more your mindset grows!

It helps me become a useful member in society.

It helps turn my dream into reality.

I can have a happy and stable life.

Help my country with economic growth.

I can earn my own money.

It makes me self-dependent.

I will not be easily fooled or cheated.

Makes me confident.

I will be able to play a major role in women empowerment.

Education Levels

Judge

Doctor

Doctoral degree

Master's degree

2-and 4-year college degree

college

Vocational Training

High School

Graduation

A graduation is a special ceremony at a university, college, or school, at which degrees and diplomas are given to students who have successfully completed their studies.

A kindergarten graduation is such a special moment in the life of a child. Marking a transition from primarily play-focused learning in nursery school and pre-kindergarten, kindergarten graduation ceremonies help children transition to more traditional, seatwork-oriented learning in first grade.

Take a moment to celebrate what you've achieved so far and appreciate the memories that this part of your education has given you. Your graduation ceremony will become an important part of your life. This is a symbol of change and progress. You are moving on to new adventures.

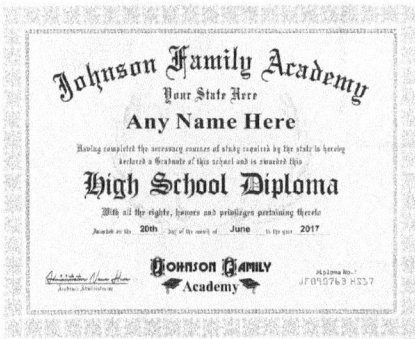

high school diploma

diploma

Kindergarten

Elementary

Middle School

High School

Educational Requirements: What does it take?

A high school diploma is the degree that you earn after you complete kindergarten through 12th grade.

Jobs you can get with a high school diploma:

Restaurant server
Movie theater clerk
Restaurant cook
Pharmacy technician
Salesperson
Mail carrier
Postal worker
Police officer
Subway operator
Security guard

Military enlisted service member
Photographer
Garbage collector
Artist
Actor
Musician

Vocational schools, or trade schools, offer short-term training that is focused on one specific career. At the end of the training, students are awarded a vocational certificate which certifies them to obtain a certain job. For example, attending truck driving vocational school prepares students to be a truck driver.

Jobs you can get with vocational training:

Electrician
Automotive technician
Carpenter
Fitness trainer
Manicurist
Medical assistant
Truck driver
Real estate agent
Detective
Radiology technician
Construction worker
Aircraft mechanic

Air traffic controller
Brick mason
Massage therapist
Software developer
Dental hygienist
Pilot
Plumber
Paralegal
Welder
Hair stylist
Cosmetologist
Paramedic

Some colleges want you to be there and study for 2 years. These colleges are called a community college, or a junior college, or a technical college. When you finish a 2-year college, you will get a degree called an Associate degree or a certificate. Some careers that you can have are: preschool teacher, police officer, secretary.

Some colleges want you to study there for 4 years in order to finish. When you finish a 4-year college, you will get a degree called a Bachelor's degree. Some careers that you need a 4-year college are: nurse, high school teacher, engineer.

Jobs you can get with a 2-and-4-year college degrees

Teacher
Mechanical engineer
Military officer
Accountant
Nurse
Computer programmer
Web designer
Nutritionist
Interior designer
Architect
Forest ranger
Chef
Journalist
Zookeeper
Fashion designer
Scientist
Chemical engineer
Sales manager

Actuary
Stock broker
Nuclear engineer
Public relations specialist
Aerospace engineer
Financial manager
Marketing specialist
Petroleum engineer
Chemist
Environmental scientist
Interpreter
Social Worker
Pastor
Religious leader
Biologist
Meteorologist
Surveyor
Astronaut
Legislator

A master's degree is a degree earned by taking additional courses —for 2 or more years— in a specialized area after earning a 4-year college degree. Master's degrees provide students with an in-depth study of a professional field such as counseling, business, finance, teaching, nursing, and others.

People get a master's degree because the jobs they want require a master's degree, they want to learn more and gain more skills in a particular area. They want to earn higher salaries, and they want to have a managerial or leadership positions in their jobs.

Jobs that require a Master's degree:

School counselor
Clinical social worker
Mental health counselor
Librarian
Occupational therapist
School principal
Nurse midwife
Physician assistant
Nurse practitioner
Business manager
Community college professor

Public health specialist
School psychologist
Music therapist
Epidemiologist
Hospital administrator
School psychologist

A doctoral degree is a highly specialized degree that is earned after completing an undergraduate, or 4-year college degree program. A doctoral degree typically takes longer to earn than a master's degree and provides a more in-depth study of the career field. A doctoral degree typically takes 3-5 years to complete, depending on the program of study.

Jobs that require a doctoral degree:

General surgeon
Judge
Lawyer
Dentist
Pharmacist
Family doctor
Veterinarian
College professor
Dentist

All medical doctors receive a doctoral degree, but many other professionals receive different types of doctoral degrees. While we may not call them doctors, lawyers and judges also receive doctoral degrees for the time they study in law school. College professors and other researchers also receive doctoral degrees in their fields of study.

College Bound - What is College?

After elementary school, you will go to middle school. Then you will go to high school. College is a place where you go to learn. Many students go to college after high school. You need to finish high school if you want to go to college. A college is also called a university.

College is very different from the school you go to now. In college, you get to pick most of what you want to learn. You will get a different teacher for every class. Your teachers in college are called professors or instructors.

Many students live at their college. Some colleges have places for their students to live. You do not have to live at your college if you want to live at home. You can drive there in a car, take a bus, or get a ride if your college is close to your home.

University of Liberia

To be successful in college, you must study hard and be responsible. You will need to become good at important skills.

| Study Hard. |
| Ask for Help. |
| Wake up on Time. |

When I think, I am exercising my brain.

| Choose the right friends. |
| Manage your money. |
| Say 'No' to negetive peer pressure. |

| Go to Class on Time. | Make healthy choices. | Do your laundry. |

Who will help you prepare for college?

Parents	Teachers	School Counselor

Going to college is very expensive. It can cost a lot of money. When the time comes if you decide if you want to go to college, you will have the choice to pay for college:

Scholarship - money that you get for college from your government, a company or a group. A scholarship is given to someone who has done very well in high school. The group will offer you a scholarship to pay for some or all of your college cost. Scholarships are given to students who make very good grades. You do not have to pay this money back.

Loans - money that is borrowed from someone or the bank to pay for all or some of your college cost. This money has to be pay back.

Cash - money that you already have to pay for college. Maybe your parents have saved money ahead of time to pay for your college. Or, you can get a job in college and use the money from your job to pay for college.

scholorship

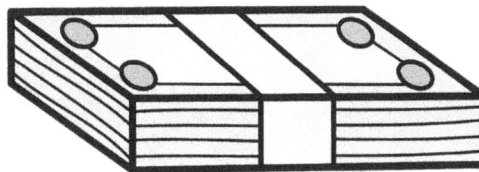

loan

cash

Save Money and Make Good Grades

Paying for college is very difficult for many families. Working hard to get good grades can help you get scholarships. Work hard and form good study habits now, so when the time comes to get scholarships, it will be easy for you.

Why Should I go to College?

Some children like school. They enjoy learning. They like to read, study, and go to school. Not everyone like school. If you don't like school, thinking about going to college might be difficult for you. Even if you don't like to read, there are a lot of good reasons why you should think about college.

If You Go To College . . .

You get to choose what you want to learn about.

You will learn to become a responsible adult.

You will become more independent and mature.

You will be able to live on your own.

You will make new friends.

You can explore many different topics, cultures, relationships, and friendships you did not know before.

Most people who have a college degree make more money than they would have made if they didn't go to college.

college campus building

University of Liberia

Choosing a College

Choosing the right college for you will depend on what you want to study and what things you want to study there. Not every college will have the things you want to study. You will need to do some research on each college and find out everything about the school before you decide.

✓ Look at the school website.
✓ Talk to people who have gone to that college
✓ Find out if that college has the major that you want to study.
✓ Find out how much it cost to go to that college.
✓ Find out if you can pay for that college.
✓ Make a list of colleges that have all the things you want.

Once you decide which colleges you like best, you will need to apply to those colleges.

What is a Major?

You will take a lot of classes in college, like you do right now. You will take math, music, science, social studies and art. You will be asked what you want to learn about the most. This is called your major. Once you decide on your major, you can take mostly classes that you want to learn about.

If someone want to be a teacher, they will have a major in education. Most of the classes they take will teach them how to teach children.

If someone wants to be a writer, they will major in journalism. Most of the classes they take will teach them how to be a great writer.

Right now you have a school counselor and teacher who help you with studying and learning. In college, you will have many teachers. You will also have a counselor to give you advice and guide you through college. This person is called your advisor. She or he will help you choose classes you want to take. Your advisor will keep track of your grades. He or she will get you help if you are having trouble in your classes. Your advisor will know a lot about your major. It is their job to help you.

Applying to College

To apply to college means to give information about yourself, and hope that you will be accepted to come to that college. You must fill out an application. A college application is a form that you fill out that tells the college about you.

A college application will ask for things like:

✓ Your name and address,
✓ Your parent's information
✓ Your test grades
✓ Your sports and activities
✓ Your interests
✓ You may also be asked to write an essay.

The Admission Office at a college is responsible for telling people about their school and deciding who can come to their college.

Someone to works at the admission office at a college will look at your application and decide if you are a good choice for their college. The person reading your application will be trying to find out what type of student you are. If they like your application, you will receive a Letter of Acceptance. If they feel that you are not a good choice, you will receive a Letter of Denial.

```
G  V  T  K  H  M  R  J  K  T  C  Q  B  B  G
M  D  P  H  R  E  F  E  R  E  N  C  E  S  R
Y  L  D  R  R  T  G  Z  S  T  N  A  R  G  M
Q  P  S  N  O  W  S  T  L  U  S  E  R  Y  K
U  I  R  T  O  F  E  C  H  O  I  C  E  R  P
E  H  E  F  D  I  E  I  T  L  W  L  Q  E  L
S  S  W  G  L  R  T  S  V  W  K  G  U  T  N
T  R  S  L  P  Z  K  A  S  E  Q  M  A  T  E
I  A  N  K  C  C  C  L  M  O  R  P  L  E  S
O  L  A  R  E  I  O  G  D  R  R  N  I  L  S
N  O  P  H  G  O  R  S  E  E  O  N  F  B  A
S  H  C  O  H  A  D  P  C  X  C  F  Y  L  Y
T  C  L  C  D  P  O  L  M  O  V  I  N  M  N
H  S  S  E  P  R  I  N  T  C  R  K  D  I  W
L  N  L  T  T  X  Q  D  H  F  W  E  R  E  F
```

Find these
"College Application"
words in the puzzle.

ANSWERS	REPORT
CHECK	RESULTS
CHOICE	REVIEW
DECIDE	SCHOLARSHIP
ESSAY	SCHOOL
GRADE	SCORE
GRANTS	TEST
INFORMATION	
LETTER	
LOGIC	
PRINT	
PROFESSOR	
QUALIFY	
QUESTIONS	
REFERENCES	

My College Application

Name:
Address:
Phone Number:
Email:
Parents / Guardian's Name:
What activities are you involve in?
What sports do you play?
What major do you want to study?
Have you ever been in trouble at school? If so, explain:
Write a paragraph telling why you should be admitted to this college:
Will you live on campus?
What kind of roommate would you like?

Have your parents attended college?
How do you intend to pay for college?
Would you like to have a job on campus to help pay for college?
Is there anything else about you that you would like the Admission Office to know?
Sign your name:

More College?

Getting a Master's and Advance Degree

There are some jobs that require you to go to school again, after you finish college. If you go to school after you finish college, you will be getting an advance degree. These are often called master's degrees.

There are other advance degrees too! Some careers that require an advance degrees are:
- ✓ Accountant
- ✓ Principal
- ✓ Doctor
- ✓ Lawyer
- ✓ College Professor
- ✓ Judge

To become a lawyer, you need an advance degree called a Juris Doctor (J.D.)

To become a medical doctor, you need to go to medical school for many years to get a degree called a M.D. or an O.D.

Even after getting a master's degree, there is still more learning to get! You can go to school again and get a doctorate. A doctorate degree is a special degree that very few people get. It requires a lot of studying in a specific study.

Having a doctorate degree does not mean you are a medical doctor. It means you have reached the highest level of education that someone in your field can have. Most doctorate degree is called a Ph.D.

Trade Schools

There are many choices you can make after high school. College is just one choice. Some people go to a trade school to learn a skill. Some people don't go to school after high school at all. Whatever you decide to do, you will need to learn new skills.

A Trade School is also known as a technical school. These schools train people to learn a trade. A trade is a job that requires a skill using your hands. At a trade school, you will learn and practice your trade.

Some examples of trades are:

✓ Nail technician
✓ Plumbing
✓ Hair styling
✓ Paramedic

Choosing a Future Career

Getting a Job

There are many jobs that do not require college or trade school. Some examples are:
- ✓ Cashier
- ✓ Bank Teller
- ✓ Custodian
- ✓ Taxi Driver

People who go to college or trade school, usually make more money than if they don't go. This is true most of the time.

Job, Career and Occupation

Job

A job is an activity, often regular and often performed in exchange for payment ("for a living"). A person begins a job by becoming an employee. The amount of time spent doing a job may range from temporary (not to last for a long time) or full-time (8-hours a day) to a lifetime career, like a judge.

Jobs can be categorized as paid or unpaid. Examples of unpaid jobs include volunteer, homemaker, mentor, and student. Did you know you already have a job? Your first job is to learn and study as a student.

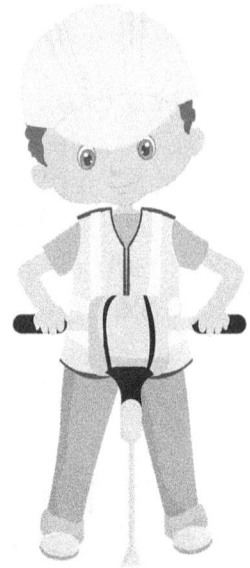

construction worker doing his job

Profession / Occupation

If a person is trained (educated) for a certain type of job, they may have a profession. A profession is the type of business a person does. It can also be called an occupation. Then usually, their job would be someone's career. One usually retires from their career. They may also leave their job, also known as resign from their job.

A lawyer is a professional who practices "law".

Career

A career is the job or profession that someone does for a long period of time in their life.

Dr. Jones had a long career in medicine.

Becoming a Community Helper

Community is a place where people live, whether it is a village or a city. We all live together in a community. We depend on one another for various necessities of life, like food or shelter. When we care for one another, we make the world a safer and more peaceful place.

Everyone who lives in a community can be a community helper. Community helpers are people who live and work in our communities. Community helpers make sure that the community stays healthy, safe and happy.

Some examples of community helpers are: doctors, nurses, chefs, bakers, astronauts, soldiers, teachers, dentists, mail carriers, bus drivers, coaches, baby sitters, fishermen, plumbers, firefighters, farmers, librarians, and volunteers.

My Dream Job

Do you like to go to school?
Do you like to study?
Do you like making good grades?
Do you like science and math?
Do you like to fix things?
Do you like to know how things work?
Do you have a clever way of doing things?
Do you like to tell stories?
Do you like to solve problems?
Do you like to teach?
Do you like to lead your friends?
Do you like to draw?
Do you like to help other people?
Do you like to sing?
Do you like to build things?

I would like to work:

☐ Indoors	☐ Outdoors
☐ Small Groups	☐ Large Groups
☐ Mornings	☐ Nights
☐ With People	☐ With Animals
☐ In a Uniform	☐ Not in Uniform
☐ Retail	☐ Office
☐ Noisy Place	☐ Quiet Place
☐ Part-Time	☐ Full-Time

Activists

You don't have to wait until you are an adult to change the world. Activism is action to make a change, or stop a change, in society. It can be trying to make a government change its laws, or trying to make people change what they do. There are many forms of activism. An activist is someone who works to bring about political or social change. When you think about "activism", you might visualize people who were arrested for trying to change an unjust law. Maybe you think of folks who join in marches, pickets, or protests.

Activism for kids has many benefits. It is a way for children and teens to learn important concepts while helping someone or something in the world. Youth activists begin to develop leadership and collaboration skills while opening their minds and providing them with purpose.

A good activist should be able to inspire other people, should believe in every word he says and should really love what he's doing. In this case he'll be very loyal to the idea.

Activists participate in some form of action to enact social or political change. These actions can range from simple things, such as letter-writing campaigns or boycotts of certain products, to participation in public protests.

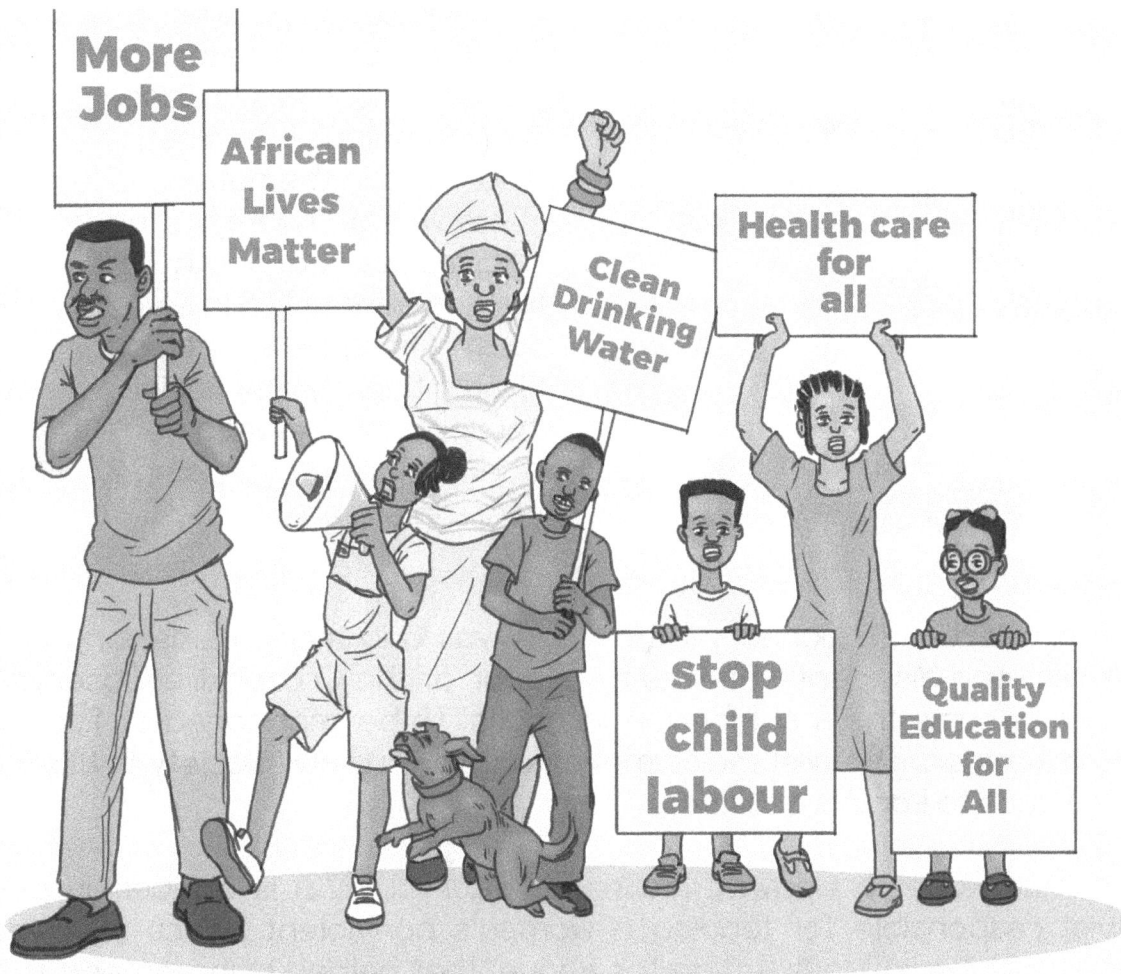

These famous activists shaped the world we live in today, thanks to their dedication to organize, speak out, and demand change.

Malala Yousafzai is the youngest person to win the Nobel Prize. She works to make sure that girls around the world can all go to school. Malala was born in Pakistan, where many girls were not allowed to go to school. She spoke out against this and was shot for it. Malala survived and still fights for girls to be able to go to school and be treated the same as boys.

Nelson Mandela was the first democratic leader of South Africa, but before that he spent 20 years in prison for campaigning against Apartheid in the nation.

He was a Civil Rights leader and President of South Africa. He was born in 1918 in Mvezo, South Africa. He spent his life fighting against racial segregation. He became president after spending 27 years in prison.

Albert Porte - (19 January 1906 – 1986) was an Americo-Liberian political journalist and dissident who was the editor of the Crozerville Observer. In 1946, he became the first Liberian journalist to be imprisoned by President William Tubman. The first major movement toward civil society in Liberia is traced back to Porte's activities.

Leymah Roberta Gbowee (born February 1, 1972) is a Liberian peace activist responsible for leading a women's nonviolent peace movement, Women of Liberia Mass Action for Peace, that helped bring an end to the Second Liberian Civil War in 2003.

Ambassador

An ambassador is someone who is sent as the chief representative of his or her government in another country. The ambassador speaks to officials of the other country about any problems and issues between the two countries. An ambassador is the President's highest-ranking representative to a specific nation or international organization abroad.

Ambassadors of Liberia are persons nominated as ambassadors by the President to serve as Liberia diplomats to individual nations of the world, to international organizations, and as ambassadors-at-large. Their appointment needs to be confirmed by the Liberian Senate.

Ambassadors do not have to pay for their oversees housing.

African Union

Artist

What do you call an artist who paints? Do you call yourself a Painter or an Artist? The problem with calling yourself a painter is that some people will think you mean someone who paints walls, as in painting houses and buildings.

An artist is a person who creates art. An artist creates works of art on a variety of surfaces, from traditional canvas, wood, and paper, to the sides of buildings. They typically use watercolor, acrylic, or oil paints to complete their work

Professional artists rely on their own artistic talent, but the best way to begin training is with a degree in fine art. Painters learn and improve their skills through repetition and practice.

Every artist needs a professional portfolio — a collection of his or her best paintings to show potential patrons and clients.

Art promotes self-esteem.

artist tools

Astronaut

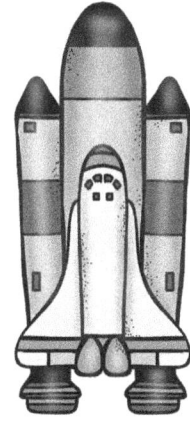

shuttle

An astronaut is a person who is specially trained to travel into outer space. Astronauts have to undergo extensive training and testing before they can participate in a spaceflight.

Astronauts are very important because they discover things in outer space such as new planets and new life. Several countries have worked together to build an International Space Station where people stay and work in space for long periods of time.

Training to become an astronaut is quite difficult and demanding. **Mission Specialist** astronauts work with pilots to conduct experiments, launch satellites, and maintain spacecraft and equipment. Their background can be in engineering, science, or medicine. They can also work as astronaut educators, inspiring students to consider joining any international space program.

Requires a bachelor's degree from a recognized university in engineering, science, physics, chemistry, biology, mathematics, or computer science. Possessing a master's degree or a doctorate helps.

satellite

Barber & Hairdresser

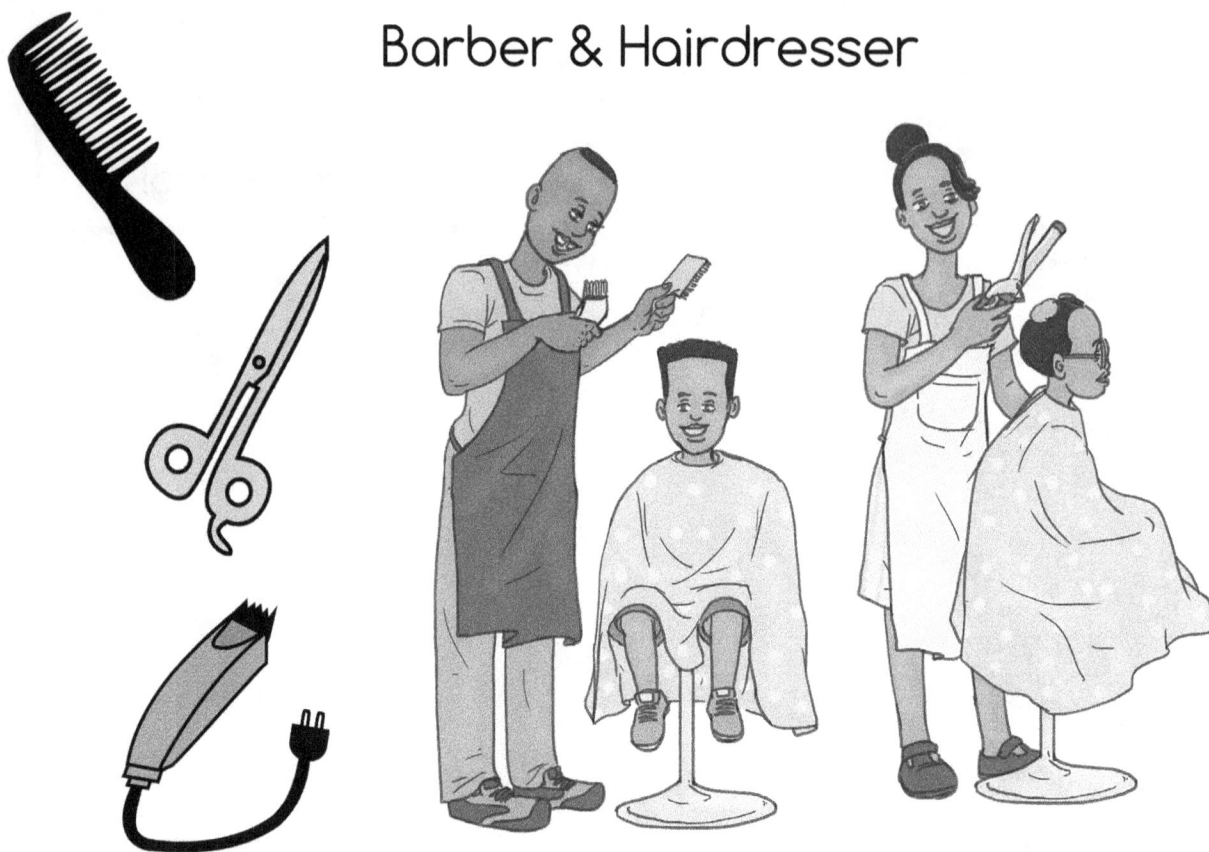

Is there a special place you go to get your haircut? If you are a boy, perhaps you visit a barbershop. If you are a girl, maybe you go to a salon. Hairdressers can work on males and females. A hairdresser and barber do much more than just cut hair.

Barbers work in a barbershop.
Hairdressers can work in a salon.
Both can also work from home.

Hairdressers apply their talents and skills of styling hair. Some are trained to braid hair or add extensions. They can dye and color hair. Hairdressers can make curly hair straight and make straight hair curly. Most can even style hair to look like a famous person's haircut. Some hairdressers work at fancy spas, shops, or salons.

Like all hairdressers, barbers also have many talented skills. Unlike hairdressers, almost all barbers are men. They cut hair for males of all ages. They show their skills with a razor. Barbers trim beards and mustaches. They also shave bald heads because most men desire clean-cut short hair. So, a barber can do dozens of haircuts a day. While a hairdresser can take hours on one hairdo. Why do you believe droves of men and women go to barbers or hairdressers?

Cameraman

A camera operator records the visual images that make up movies, television shows, news broadcasts, music videos and televised news and sporting events. If you were to visit the set of a movie or television show, you would see the "cameraman" filming the action.

Being a cameraman is exciting, but it does have its moments of being tired and boring. It's a unique career choice for someone who is physical, focused and likes to be around action. Camera operators use digital equipment to capture live action.

A cameraman's top responsibilities are to operate a camera and to shoot video, collaborate with the director and production team, assist with lighting and sound setup, frame camera shots, and edit film.

To be a successful cameraman, you'll need three key things:

- ✓ Train as a cameraman at a film school.
- ✓ Successfully complete internship as a cameraman.
- ✓ Find a job as a cameraman.

cameraman camera

Chef

tools a chef needs

tools a chef needs

Do you want to be a chef when you grow up? Anyone can go to school to become a chef. Some chefs can also become famous for their recipes. If you become a popular chef, you can have a special dish named after yourself or even your own television show!

Chefs are people who cook. Some chefs work in restaurants. Most chefs are professional cooks. They may even attend school to become an expert at cooking. If you like to cook maybe you can be a chef.

Chefs use ingredients to cook delicious dishes for others to eat. A chef usually becomes a pro at cooking a special style of food. Some chefs might cook only African or Italian food. There are chefs who fry, bake, or grill.

Do you know anyone who is a chef?

52

Who Bakes?

People love the smell of freshly baked goods. Bakers have a job that has been around for hundreds of years. A baker is someone who bakes cakes, donuts, cookies, or breads. There are many kinds of bakers.

There are bakers that specialize in just breads like sandwich bread, dinner rolls, and cornbread. Others, bake delectable mouth-watering goodies such as cookies, cakes, donuts, and pies. Bakers use ingredients like flour, salt, and yeast. They use an oven to bake delicious food for people to enjoy.

Bakers rise from bed long before the sun comes up to go to work in a hot bakery. Most bakeshops need to have someone come in very early to start baking. They get to work before six in the morning. Many people go to a bakery in the morning for fresh baked goods. They want fresh baked goods. Do you like to smell fresh baked goods?

Computer Technician

Techs Needed!

✓ Teaches others about computers
✓ Enjoys using technology
✓ Fixes computers
✓ Knows a lot about computers
✓ Builds computers
✓ Can work in a shop, school or many other places

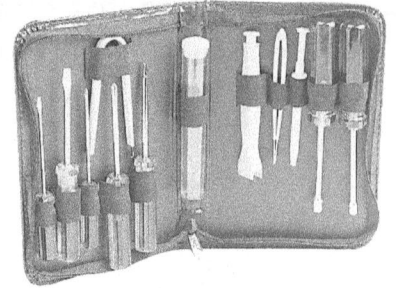

computer repair tools

Computer Mouse

Can you believe that computers are less than fifty years old? Millions of computers are made every year in factories across the world. Because so many computers are made, there is a need for computer technicians to maintain them. They fix computers when they go haywire. More people are using computers than ever. Computer technicians have a very secure career.

Technicians can program computers to fix themselves similar to how a patient listens to a doctor and takes care of themselves.

A computer technician fixes computers just like how a mechanic fixes cars. An automobile mechanic will keep cars running by changing parts and oil. A computer technician does similar work to maintain computers. They do not change oil, but upload programs and applications. Updating computers is something else they do. They even fix cracked screens and clean computers so they run properly. Like any profession, the more education a computer tech gets, the more valuable they become to consumers.

Computer technicians are also known as computer tech, tech solve problems. When was the last time you or your family had a computer problem? Did you loose anything on your computer? Computer techs are a relief because they save information. Computer techs can be mobile and some go to businesses. Many others go to houses to fix computers. Computer technicians do a valuable service for all of us.

computer repair tools

UNDER REPAIR

DO NOT USE!

Construction Worker

SAFETY HELMET

Do you enjoy building and constructing things? Have you ever thought about becoming a construction worker? Construction workers can build many things. Construction workers build a wide variety of different things! They can work with wood, metal, and other materials. Imagine if there were no construction workers to build homes or buildings? There would not be any bridges and there would not be any highways or monuments.

Just about anyone can become a construction worker. First of all, there are laborers and this is a very basic level. Many of the laborers use hammers and they work extremely hard. Next, a construction worker can become a manager and they lead the laborers. With college, a construction worker can become a designer or engineer. In the end, they will make the plans to build structures.

Have you ever taken the time to build something that broke or fell? Building can be a very dangerous job. Construction workers have to be cautious. They must follow codes. Following the rules protects them. Construction workers use safety gear. In 1920, they started wearing yellow hard hats. This tradition continues today.

Dentist

What Dentist Do?

Many people do not enjoy visiting the dentist office. A dentist is a doctor whose job is to care for teeth. They help people who might have something wrong with their teeth. A problem people can have wrong with their teeth could be cavities. Cavities are holes in teeth that can cause people agonizing pain.

Dentists want everyone to brush and floss their teeth at least twice a day. Dentists truly want people to keep their teeth clean.

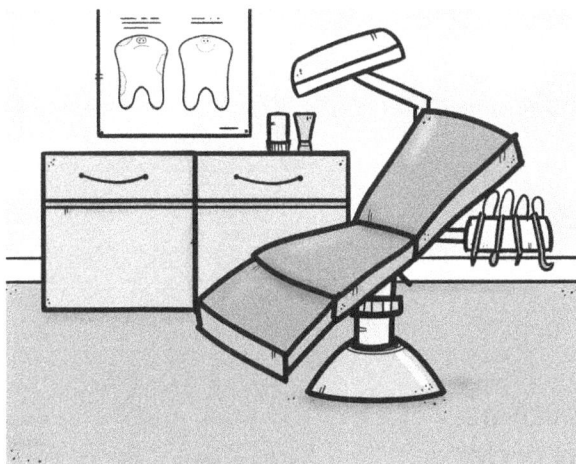

Tooth decay can happen when plaque builds up. Plaque is a thin, sticky layer that covers teeth that causes cavities. To prevent plaque from forming on teeth people must brush and floss. A dentist can make a lot of money when they do their job. People pay a lot of money to have their cavities fixed.

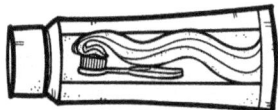

A dental operation can cost thousands of dollars.

Do you want to be a dentist when you grow up?

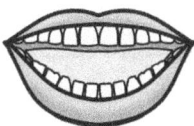

Detective

A detective is a person who investigates crime. Their job is to discover what has happened in a crime or other situation and to find the people involved. Most detectives are police officers. Some are hired by a private person or company, for example to stop theft. Detectives will search public and private databases, investigate people and examine evidence in order to solve the case.

Detectives spend much of their time interviewing suspects and witnesses, collecting evidence and testifying in court. They also arrest criminals and fugitives. The work can be dangerous. Detectives must file reports of their activities, which means they have many hours of paperwork.

Police and detectives maintain law and order.

✓ ASKS QUESTIONS.
✓ LIKES A CHALLENGE.
✓ STUDIES FINGERPRINTS AND EVIDENCE.
✓ CONDUCTS INTERVIEWS.
✓ EXAMINES CRIME SCENES.
✓ LOOKS FOR CLUES.
✓ USES THEIR FIVE SENSES.
✓ KEEPS RECORDS.
✓ SOLVES PROBLEMS AND CRIMES.

fingerprint

Doctor

A doctor is an extremely important profession. Did you know that the most needed occupation in the world is a doctor? There are some places that do not even have doctors. Most people need doctors to keep them healthy. Doctors are like scientists. They use science to figure out why their patients are sick.

A couple of jobs that a doctor has is to fix broken bones and give us medicines. Many people would be hurt for a long time without doctors. It takes an astronomical amount of schooling to become a doctor. Some doctors never stop going to school. They get educated to help patients. By going to school they learn new ways to help their patients. They often use computers and other things like robots to perform operations. Doctors do a wide variety of different jobs. Some doctors only work with patients that are sick. Other doctors can fix only one part of your body while some doctors only work on heads, like a brain surgeon. Many people get sick or hurt every day, so we need more doctors to help people.

Some tools in a Doctor's bag.

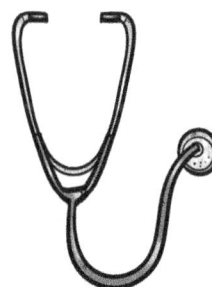

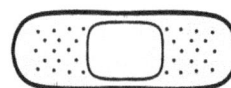

Eye Doctor

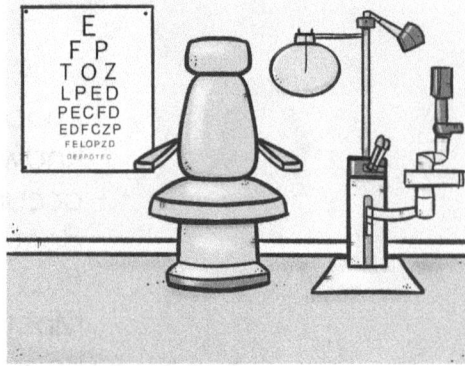

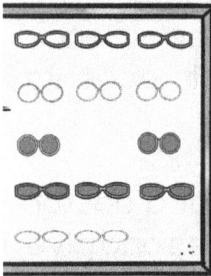

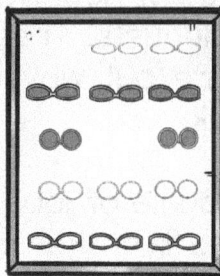

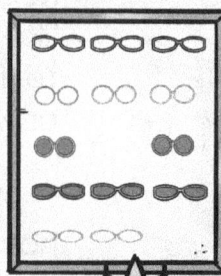

eye doctor waiting room

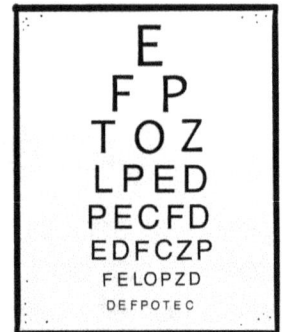

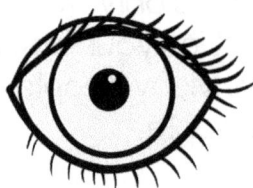

ophthalmoscope

Eye Drops

An eye doctor is called an ophthalmologist. An ophthalmologist diagnoses and treats all eye diseases, performs eye surgery and prescribes and fits eyeglasses and contact lenses to correct vision problems.

Optometrists, ophthalmologists, and opticians are all professionals who specialize in eye care. An optometrist is an eye doctor that can examine, diagnose, and treat your eyes. An ophthalmologist is a medical doctor who can perform medical and surgical interventions for eye conditions. Opticians are technicians trained to design, verify and fit eyeglass lenses and frames, contact lenses, and other devices to correct eyesight. They use prescriptions supplied by ophthalmologists or optometrists, but do not test vision or write prescriptions.

What Doctor Will You Be?

Learn about the different types of doctors.

ALLERGIST
ANESTHESIOLOGIST
CARDIOLOGIST
DERMATOLOGIST
ENDOCRINOLOGIST
GASTROENTEROLOGIST
GENETICIST
GYNECOLOGIST
HEMATOLOGIST
INTERNIST
NEPHROLOGIST

NEUROLOGIST
ONCOLOGIST
OPHTHALMOLOGIST
OSTEOPATH
OTOLARYNGOLOGIST
PATHOLOGIST
PEDIATRICIAN
PHYSIATRIST
PODIATRIST
PSYCHIATRIST
PULMONOLOGIST

RADIOLOGIST
RHEUMATOLOGIST
UROLOGIST

```
P  H  Y  S  I  A  T  R  I  S  T  T  D  L  T  W  G  Q  T  G  T  K  R
T  S  I  G  O  L  O  G  N  Y  R  A  L  O  T  O  N  W  S  S  E  G  Z
B  M  H  C  A  R  D  I  O  L  O  G  I  S  T  R  L  R  I  L  N  A  P
T  T  S  I  G  O  L  O  T  A  M  U  E  H  R  M  D  G  G  J  D  S  S
L  S  D  B  L  C  P  R  X  J  G  L  B  F  R  K  O  M  O  T  O  T  Y
T  K  I  X  D  Y  K  R  T  E  G  N  X  A  K  L  M  O  L  F  C  R  C
K  S  Q  G  G  E  F  Y  N  S  G  R  D  K  O  F  S  T  O  M  R  O  H
L  R  I  B  O  L  R  E  G  L  I  I  T  I  Y  T  M  N  M  H  I  E  I
M  O  G  G  Z  L  T  M  J  D  O  G  S  N  E  H  T  J  L  C  N  N  A
M  X  N  R  O  I  O  M  A  L  P  E  O  O  L  R  P  X  A  G  O  T  T
K  H  B  C  C  L  H  T  O  T  H  O  P  L  M  B  K  L  H  T  L  E  R
Z  Y  T  I  O  T  O  G  A  T  O  A  D  N  O  T  X  K  T  Z  O  R  I
J  N  S  T  P  L  I  H  S  M  T  L  A  I  S  R  R  N  H  M  G  O  S
T  T  I  S  T  S  O  E  T  H  E  I  O  I  A  L  U  L  P  K  I  L  T
J  B  N  I  T  K  N  G  L  A  C  H  G  G  T  T  X  R  O  M  S  O  X
R  H  R  G  P  A  H  G  I  I  P  O  J  K  I  R  R  C  Z  D  T  G  R
W  R  E  R  N  K  T  K  R  S  L  L  P  K  N  S  R  I  Q  K  F  I  J
R  W  T  E  K  Z  Q  T  K  O  T  F  B  N  T  B  T  H  S  Q  B  S  H
L  N  N  L  J  K  A  P  R  N  T  D  T  L  W  H  X  T  H  T  N  T  P
G  V  I  L  M  I  T  H  X  T  S  I  G  O  L  O  C  E  N  Y  G  N  K
D  C  N  A  D  R  P  H  C  R  N  D  K  M  F  K  G  H  Y  J  Y  T  C
Q  R  M  E  L  E  P  T  S  I  G  O  L  O  N  O  M  L  U  P  L  H  L
V  Q  P  P  N  N  G  R  N  X  N  E  U  R  O  L  O  G  I  S  T  M  Q
```

Engineering

An engineer is someone who designs, builds, or maintains machines, engines, structures, and even the environment. They help create everything around us. Engineers want to know how and why things work. They have scientific training that they use to make practical things.

Some different types of engineers include: Structural Engineers, Civil Engineers, Electrical Engineers, Mechanical Engineers, Chemical Engineers, Environmental Engineers, Manufacturing Engineers, Systems Engineers, and Material Scientists.

The Engineering Design Process is a step-by-step process that engineers use to solve problems not easy to understand or explain.

We are engineers when we use the engineering process:

Ask
Imagine
Plan
Create
Test
Improve
Share

The Engineering Process

When I ASK a question:
I state the problem in my own words, and I define the criteria that must be met or a successful solution. Criteria means a standard by which something can be judge.

When I IMAGINE possible solutions:
I think about the strengths and weaknesses of more than one idea.

When I PLAN my design:
I use prior knowledge and the challenge criteria to create a written plan that includes a diagram and a supplies list

When I CREATE a prototype: prototype is an original or first model of something from which other forms are copied or developed.
I use my plan as a blueprint to build a prototype or model. I choose appropriate tools, follow safety rules, and adapt my plan as needed.

When I TEST my prototype:
I evaluate my prototype using the challenge criteria. I notice any problem or possible improvements.

When I IMPROVE my design:
I make changes to make my prototype better. I brainstorm ideas for more improvements, even if I don't have the needed time or materials.

I often SHARE my work:
I work with others. I respectfully give and receive feedback as I work. I will speak and write about what I built.

What would you build for your community?
A bridge?
A tall building?

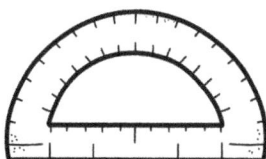

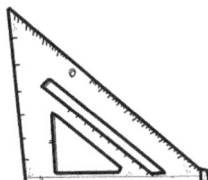

Farmer

There are many different kinds of farmers. They specialize in different areas. Some farmers grow fruit or vegetables. Other farmers may work with animals like cows, chickens, and pigs.

People rely on farming to feed their families. For a long time, farmers use traditional tools to make rows prior to planting. Using hand tools for farming means taking too long to produce food and extra hard labor. To produce more food with less labor, farmers are turning to technology.

Technology on the Farm - today, people use machines and computers to help make the job of farming easier. Technology helps farmers work faster and more effectively. They use tractors to plow fields. Using sophisticated tools in farming helps to reduce poverty and boost economic growth.

What farmer
are you going to be?

Farm Tools & Equipments

Axe
Baskets
Bolo
Chainsaw
Coat
Crowbar
Cutlass
Fishing nets
Garden Hoe
Gloves
Hat
Head lamp
Hook and Line

Housing (cage)
Jig Saw
Lantern
Meat Scale
Pickup truck
Pocket knife
Post hole Digger
Produce Scale
Rubber Boots
Screwdriver
Shovel
Soil Blocker
Tiller

Tractor
Traps
Watering can
Wheelbarrow

```
W A T E R I N G C A N W A S G I J W K M M W
K B Q N T R A P S X C T T R N E T R T Q H H
Y P H G R S A L T U C Y B Q O K N F N M O
R Y R E C E N T R L M G E X H H T T G N L O
H A T X A N T Z K E R R X G L N T B N H V K
P T M D P D N N K Q K V A V V E F Z Z P P A
O V B N B Z L L A W Z C K P R D Q Q Q B W N
S W S L R X N A S L Q C O O T R T L K V Q D
T Z C N C C Y E M K X C T L S A K W N C H L
H V R M L H V R P P N C H T B G Z F M O C I
O V E N Y O J W L R A T E A M L R Q U L R N
L B W R L N S B H R O K V D I K I S M U T E
E P D G M R M T T E S D C Z C N I O B T E K
D N R L K E J Z E A E R U U L N S B S N L N
I V I F Q L R L B N O L R C G G E A K T A Y
G Y V M V L H C W W G T B ( E R F Y W R C L
G C E Z D I F O B C P N C A B S K K M M S V
E K R Q N T X A K U M A I O R X C L Y M T R
R W L X N K R T K R G M O H T R D A T F A J
L E V O H S R C M E C T J T S G O Q L B E J
M W B O L O I L ) T S L M C T I T W F E M T
L P L G P P W P O C K E T K N I F E D Z T T
```

65

Flight Attendant

Flight Attendants are responsible for making sure passengers are safe and comfortable at all times. Their duties include making sure that the emergency equipment is working, that the cabin is clean, and that there is enough supply of food and beverages.

Flight Attendants greet passengers, help them find their seats and stow their bags, serve meals, and cope with turbulence, airsickness, and disruptive travelers.

Flight attendants have variable work schedules, including evenings, weekends, and holidays, because airlines operate every day and some offer overnight flights. They work in an aircraft and may be away from home several nights per week.

During their time off, most airlines allow flight attendants to fly for free on what's called "stand-by". This means that as a flight attendant you get to use those free tickets if there is available seat on the flight.

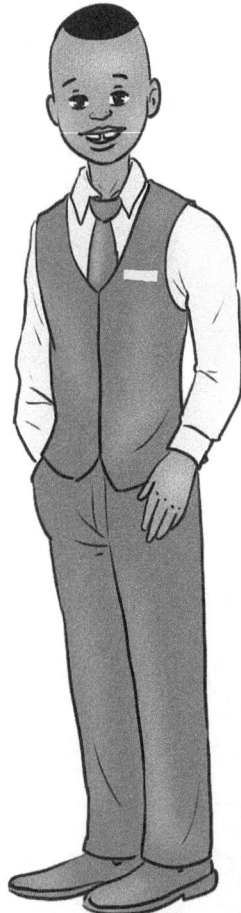

Firefighter

Did you know that people used to put out fires with buckets of water? People started building fire departments to fight fires. In the beginning, the first firefighters were volunteers. There is always a constant threat of fires. So, schools started professional fire fighting programs.

Firefighters deal with so much more than just fires. Everyday firefighters are called to duty. When there is a threat, firefighters rescue people. They also rescue animals and show up when there is an accident. Firefighters come when someone gets hurt. They are trained to provide medical care. Firefighters do their job during natural disasters like storms and earthquakes. Firefighters also inspect buildings, fire hydrants, and fire extinguishers to make sure everything is working in case of a fire.

Firefighters use many different tools during times of distress. When people are trapped in their homes, firefighters rescue them with ladders, hoses, and special tools. They also have heavy equipment for different situations. Boats are used to put out fires on ships. They use planes to drop water on forest and mountain fires.

Training

Have you ever thought about becoming a firefighter? First, go to firefighter school and do your personal best. There you will have to pass many tests. When you are done you will be ready to get hired by a fire department. In the end, you will feel rewarded rescuing people from deadly fires.

What is the color
of the firefighter's uniform
in your community?

Fisherman

Fishing is the activity of trying to catch fish. Fishing can be done in the sea, or in a lake or river, and by boat, canoe, or from the shore. Working at sea can be challenging. A fisherman or fisher is a person who catches fish, and sometimes other animals that live in water. Fishermen usually catch fish so that they can sell the fish to make money. The commercial fishing and seafood industry consist of harvesters, processors, dealers, wholesalers, and retailers. Becoming a commercial fisherman and selling the product requires business and marketing skills. By apprenticing with experienced fishermen, you can gain the knowledge and skills to launch your career in fishing.

Most commercial fishermen have some sort of license to operate a boat, and most will have a financial arrangement with a fishing company to ensure they get paid for catching the fish. The fishing company then pays the fishermen for bringing in the fish and they pay them when the season is over.

A career as a fisherman is a hard one but does have many rewards.

Geologist Rocks!

Do you love playing in the dirt, digging in the sand, and splashing in the ocean? You can be a geologist when you grow up. As a geologist, you will learn all about the Earth.

A Geologist:
- ✓ Examines rocks and minerals
- ✓ Identifies landforms
- ✓ Asks questions and writes report
- ✓ Studies how the Earth was made and erodes
- ✓ Takes pictures of the Earth
- ✓ Learns about volcanoes and earthquakes

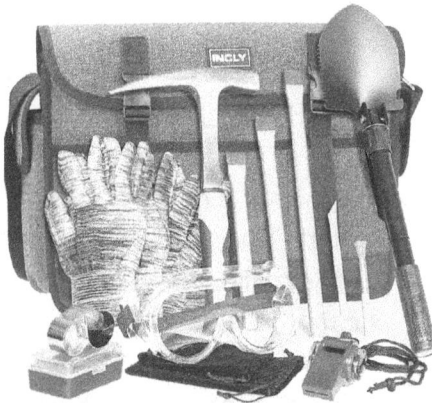

Geologist tools

Geologist tools

geologist compass

Inventor

Inventors create a solution to a real life problem. They use creative thinking to solve all types of problems. What they all have in common is an idea and a vision to deliver what they felt would make the world a better place.

Fine the last names of these famous inventors in the puzzle below.

> "I didn't fail the test, I just found 100 ways to do it wrong."
> -Benjamin Franklin

> "Education is the key to unlock the golden door of freedom."
> -George W. Carver

BENJAMIN BANNEKER
BENJAMIN FRANKLIN
CARLOS FINLAY
ELI WHITNEY
GARRETT MORGAN
George Washington CARVER
HENRY FORD
JAMES NAISMITH
JOHANNES GUTENBERG
LEONARDO DA VINCI
LEVI STRAUSS
LOUIS BRAILLE
LOUIS PASTEUR
MADAM C.J. WALKER
MARIE CURIE
MARY ANDERSON
NIKOLA TESLA
RUTH HANDLER
RUTH WAKEFIELD
SAMUEL MORSE
SARAH E. GOODE
STEVE JOBS
THOMAS EDISON
TIM BERNERS-LEE
WILLEM J. KOLFF
WRIGHT BROTHERS

```
E P M R H A N D L E R K F J J N F A
Z I M Y G Z G C V P J N N J M M L G
M C R D L E I F E K A W O J G S L G
D T Y U F W P M M Z K B W R E P R E
K R N L C I F T X W S M E T A E E S
Z G O F R A N K L I N K T S B L N R
H O K F X T R L M C E W T N S M F E
Y O R E V R A C A N M E E R N H K H
L D T Q K W M Z N Y U T E M O T T T
W E L B K H N A T R U N O W S I T O
W V L V Y I B B L G R R C B R M R R
S B E X X T H R N E G M Y K E S D B
N T B Q G N T A B A X K L C D I H T
F M R L F E F I N K V K W C N A V H
G F O A C Y R L R E K L A W A N H G
Y W L R U X C L E D I S O N M N G I
R X Y O S S L E D A V I N C I C M R
W D R L K E S C N N M R V B Q M Q W
```

Inventions That Changed the World

Fine the list of things invented that changed the world.

ABACUS
AIRPLANE
ANESTHESIA
AUTOMOBILE
CAMERA
CAR
CEMENT
CLOCK
COMPASS
COMPUTER
ELECTRICITY

INTERNET
IPOD
KEY
LAPTOP
LIGHT BULB
PAPER
PENICILLIN
PLOW
PHOTOGRAPHY
PRINTING PRESS
RADIO

RECORD PLAYER
REFRIGERATOR
SAILBOAT
STEAM ENGINE
STEREO
TABLET
TELEGRAPH
TELEPHONE
TELESCOPE
TELEVISION
TYPEWRITER

VACCINATION
WHEEL

lightbulb

```
W N R C P R I N T I N G P R E S S L G S Y W
L Q F P F E N I G N E M A E T S R L A T G P
V P H O T O G R A P H Y K N R W K I T T R R
Q Y K M M E L E C T R I C I T Y L P E S I E
M R C T Q G P J H N A R B T G B Z Z L S P C
T T T E L E S C O P E U C W O Q M K E A O O
K C V G G L N K R C H G T A Z L M V V P D R
N N M T B M P L O W V C T O N J A X I M C D
S T E R E O H W W F P D H L M C X R S O A P
B L U B T H G I L K T Y P T C O E Q I C M L
R P F H P A N E S T H E S I A T B R O B E A
Q E P C V D L K E R N N N L U L M I N K R Y
D M F X T H Y N D I V A A P C L M Y L N A E
X I C R J L O E L R T P M M G K Q T E E H R
L A N T I H L L K I T O R T T K D N L T P L
R E Q T P G I R O O C S T A E T A K Q R A N
F T E E E C E N P R W U N J D L C N X E R T
H H L H I R H R V B R C R K P I B F T P G M
D E F N W M N T A H H A P R C R O A M A E R
T N E M E C L E K T Z B I K D O T M T P L Y
Q P B Z X V Z J T T O A M L L D L N H G E N
R E T I R W E P Y T J R W J X H L C B C T K
```

Judge

A court judge smacks a mallet called a gavel,
on the desk to keep people in order
and to make their final judgment.

Bible

gavel

the jury

Did you know that judges are like investigators who solve problems? Their duty is to make fair and just decisions. They can give people permission to build things. Judges decide punishments and uphold laws to protect people and property. Judges make sure everyone follows local and federal laws. Their purpose is to keep life civil and fair.

In order to become an official judge, a great amount of education is required. There are thousands of laws. It can take a law student over 10 years to finish college. Before anyone becomes a judge he or she is first a lawyer. Not all lawyers earn the opportunity to become a judge. Ultimately, they are selected for their fairness and honesty.

Lawyers

lady justice
statue

A LAWYER IS ALSO CALLED AN
- ✓ ADVOCATE
- ✓ ATTORNEY
- ✓ BARRISTER
- ✓ COUNSEL
- ✓ COUNSELLOR
- ✓ SOLICITOR
- ✓ PROSECUTOR

LAW

A lawyer is someone who practices law. A lawyer has earned a degree in law, and has a license to practice law in a particular area.

A legal problem is referred to as a case. If people have any problem regarding the law, they can contact a lawyer for advice. A person can hire a lawyer to start a case against someone else, or to help with a case that has been started against them. If the case goes to court, the lawyer will represent the person in court. The lawyer will use their knowledge of the law to convince the court that the client is on the right side of the argument.

When a person is accused of a crime, the person has a defense lawyer to try to show they have not committed a crime. The lawyer arguing that they did do the crime is called the prosecutor.

Lawyers generally charge a fee for the work that they do, but sometimes advice is offered freely, which is called "pro bono," meaning "for the public good."

Lawyers work in different settings. Some work by themselves, while some work in law firms. Some lawyers work for hospitals and private companies.

Mechanics

Auto mechanics are always needed because vehicles will always need maintenance and repair.

Auto Mechanics have an amazing collection of tools. If you're a hands-on person, then imagine what you can accomplish with dozens of tools at your fingertips! Start building their collection of tools while attending mechanic college.

Auto mechanics are self-reliant, you'll also be able to work on your own car. Detecting problems and doing repairs on your own car gives you the self-reliance of not having to pay anyone else to get the job done.

Auto Mechanics are knowledgeable. When you start gaining experience as an auto mechanic, you become an expert on the type of cars. Auto mechanics get asked for car advice a lot. Your knowledge can save friends and family a lot of time and money, whether or not you fix their cars for them.

Can you think of any other great reasons to become an auto mechanic?

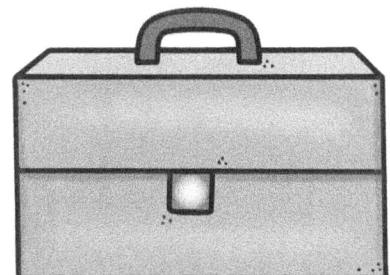

tool box

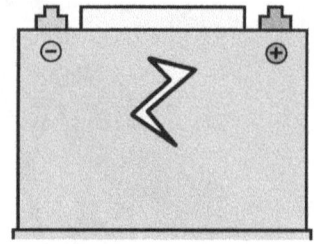

car battery

A Mechanic's Tool Collection is Never Complete!

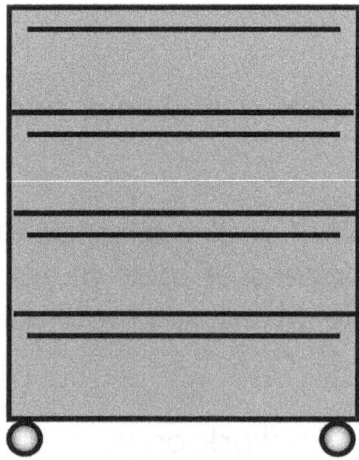

tool drawers

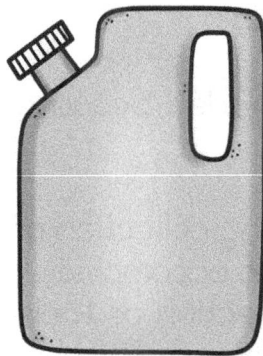

gas container

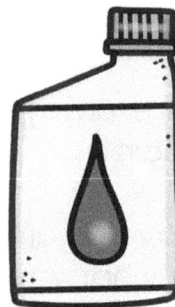

oil

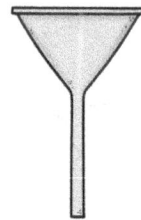

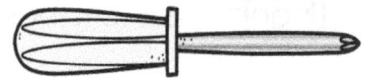

screwdriver

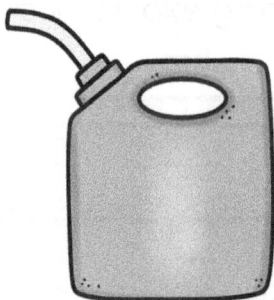

liquid container

✓ WORKS ON CARS, BOATS, AND OTHER VEHICLES
✓ MAKES THINGS RUN BETTER
✓ USES HAMMERS, WRENCHES, DRILLS, AND OTHER TOOLS
✓ LIKES TO FIX THINGS
✓ DOESN'T MIND GETTER DIRTY
✓ TAKES OFF OLD PARTS AND PUTS NEW ONES ON

76

Car Repairs

A Mechanic's Tool Collection is Never Complete!

Air compressor
Breaker bar
Code reader
Diagnostic equipment
Digital multimeter (DMM)
Fire extinguisher
Flashlight
Fluid drain pan
Funnels
Hammers
Impact wrench
Jack and jack stands

Mechanic's Stethoscope
Oil filter wrench
Pick set
Pliers
Pry bar
Punches and chisels
Ratchet and Socket set
Repair manual
Safety glasses
Scan tool
Screwdriver set
Shop equipment

Tire pressure gauge
Toolbox
Torque wrench
Wheel chocks
Wrench set

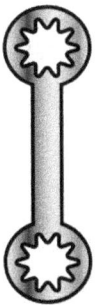

```
N R G S M F M H R K S E S S A L G Y T E F A S P S
V T S H E W L P O K T O R Q U E W R E N C H K T D
M R C O C Z Q A S I M P A C T W R E N C H D D H N
R D R P H W K R S X O K R M N V R T K X N S K P A
A I E E A Q K W E H S I J L Q Z X H V F L Q V W T
T A W Q N X G Y R J L K L S R E I L P E G H S M S
C G D U I X P L P E K I C F V T L R S G V K L C K
H N R I C T D V M K T M G O I M Q I Q R T F E T C
E O I P S E P L O R F E M H H L H D G Q M P N Q A
T S V M T S Q L C K L T M Y T C T N T T Z B N H J
A T E E E H C G R N V P C I D M L E C R Y D U D D
N I R N T C L V I M B R P N T F L E R N B T F V N
D C S T H N K L A T A I A F L L S F E W P N N Q A
S E E Z O E T X J B C S K U T M U C Z H R M Y M K
O Q T T S R R T R K E V I O M X K M A V W E P Z C
C U V N C W C E S H D D O F X G J R L N H N N T A
K I H Q O K K E C Y D L F T C S X T R A T R L C J
E P V T P A T N W R B L W K R N T X L Q T O T N H
T M V R E C U T A O C O D E R E A D E R R I O Y N
S E R R T P G I X W C H M R N T W L K N Y L G L T
E N B A K K N Q T Y N M M W Q C Y T W Y T K C I R
T T T D B P F G D C A R E P A I R M A N U A L R D
P R T C A Y P R E H S I U G N I T X E E R I F X G
F J N N T I R E P R E S S U R E G A U G E N K H T
K M Z T J Z N P N M L L F M W L W T P L P T T T T
```

Meteorologist

Have you ever watched the news with your family? If you have, then maybe you saw a man or woman reporting the weather. A meteorologist is a scientist who studies the weather and environment. They observe patterns in the weather by using tools such as computers. Meteorologists analyze the data they collect from their tools to predict the weather.

Do you like meteorology?

A meteorologist on the news will forecast the weather several times a day. Anyone who wants to become a meteorologist must go to college.

First, they must do their personal best in school and need at least four years of college. Many people go to school for much more than four years because they want to learn more about meteorology.

Can you imagine working outdoors during a thunderstorm? Many meteorologists go to places where the weather is severe. Because they are outside, they can give a first-hand account of dangerous weather.

At the very top of the list, is a chief meteorologist. Some people who watch the news admire them because they are in the newsroom. Have you ever seen someone report the weather? They are usually the chief meteorologists for the news station. If you enjoy looking at weather patterns then this is the job for you.

Musicians

Musicians write, record, and perform music. They may be trained in a particular musical genre and play a number of instruments. Musicians' daily activities include rehearsing, recording, writing lyrics and delivering performances. They may also appear on TV and radio. You must show up on time for performances, rehearsals, and studio sessions.

DJ equipment

band sound system

Nurse

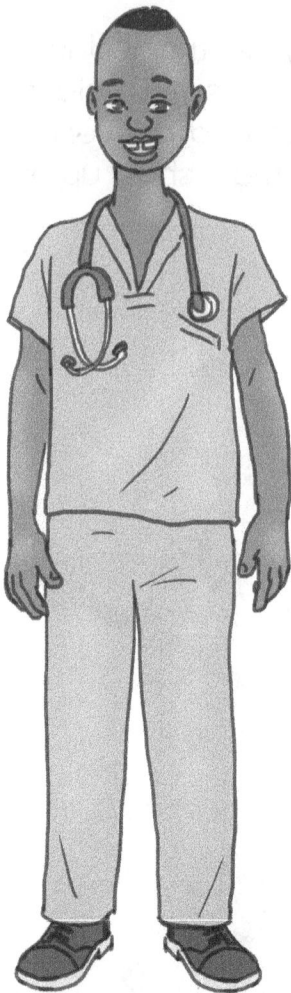

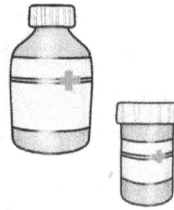

A Nurse:
- ✓ Works in hospitals, schools and doctor's offices
- ✓ Helps doctors
- ✓ Is patient and kind
- ✓ Works long hours
- ✓ Takes care of sick people
- ✓ Gives people the medicine they need
- ✓ Makes people feel better
- ✓ Wears a uniform called scrubs
- ✓ Likes helping people

Nurses come in all different colors and sizes and shapes!

A nurse encourage people to make healthy choices in all aspects of their lives, from exercise and eating right to being aware of how they can get sick. They can treat mild fevers or headaches with the use of medicines the doctor orders. Medicine is very important. Medicine is what helps people to feel better. Some pills help with pain and some help the symptoms of our sickness.

Do you like to help make people feel well? Do you want to be a nurse when you grow up?

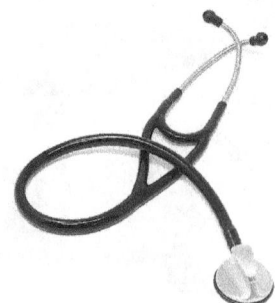

necessary tools for a nurse

Painter and Plumber

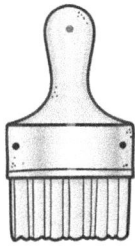

pen cutter

brush

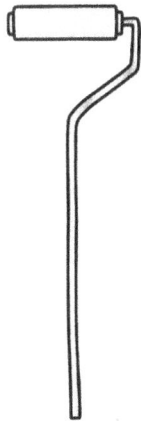

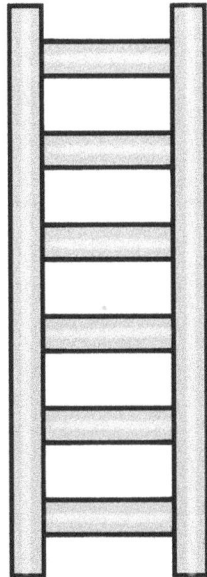

Painters work indoors and outdoors. They apply paint, stain, and coatings to walls and ceilings, buildings, large machinery and equipment, and bridges and other structures. Painting is physically demanding and requires a lot of bending, kneeling, reaching, and climbing.

The purpose of painting is to improve the appearance of a building and to protect it from damage by water, corrosion, insects and mould.

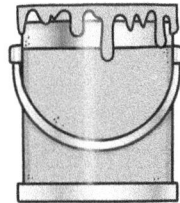

long arm roller

paint can   filler

Plumbers maintain the flow and drainage of water, air, and other gases by assembling, installing, and repairing pipes, fittings, and plumbing fixtures. They provide for the safe condition and operation of all plumbing systems.

pliers

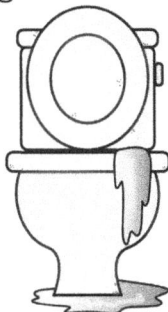

plunger

toilet overflowing

plumber van

Pharmacist

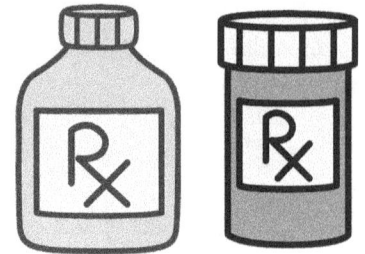

medicine-bottle

A Pharmacist:
- ✓ Is dependable
- ✓ Likes helping people
- ✓ Works in a pharmacy
- ✓ Knows a lot about medicine
- ✓ Makes sure you get the right medicine
- ✓ Works with doctors
- ✓ Has good communication skills
- ✓ Enjoys helping people
- ✓ Uses scales and computers
- ✓ Refills prescriptions

    You have to go to a School of Pharmacy and earn your Doctor of Pharmacy (or PharmD) degree.

Photographer

- ✓ Enjoys taking pictures
- ✓ Uses a camera and computer software
- ✓ Captures special moments
- ✓ Works in and out of a studio
- ✓ Works with children and adults
- ✓ Uses props and lighting
- ✓ Edits and prints photos
- ✓ Take pictures at special events, such as weddings and graduations

Pictures help people remember the past.

Do you see dollar signs ($) when people smile and say cheese! Then a job as a photographer might be right for you. "Say cheese!" This is a phrase used by many photographers. When there is a need for professional pictures, a photographer is hired. Their job is to take pictures with a camera. Capturing images is their task.

There are many different kinds of photographers. Fashion photographers may take pictures of clothes for magazines. Landscape photographers take pictures of land. Event photographers take pictures of special moments like graduations or weddings. Wildlife photographers take pictures of animals that live in the wild. Action photographers take pictures of sporting events. Today, anyone can use a cell phone to be a photographer.

Formal education is not required to become a photographer, but you will need training. Many photographers get degrees in photography, or at least take many classes in photography. Through education, training or experience, photographers need to learn about equipment, gain computer skills and understand design and picture composition. Photographers get jobs through their portfolio (a collection of their best work that they can show to possible customers).

Camera History

The camera is one of the most important inventions of all time. The camera is an incredible device that can take pictures at any moment and preserve them for all time.

Timeline of the Camera

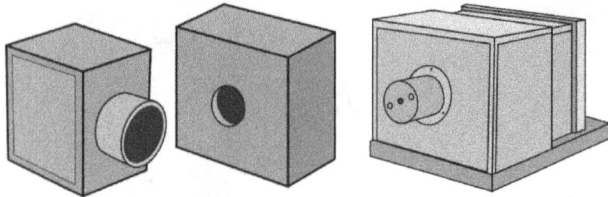

1830s Camera

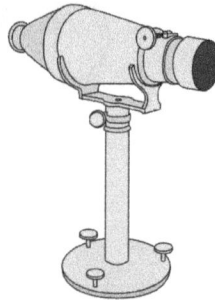

1840s Camera

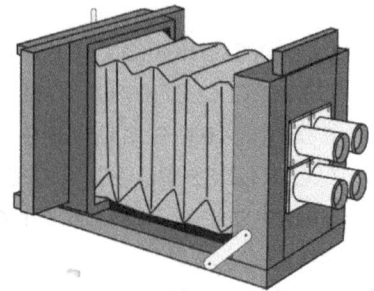

1860s Camera

1880s Camera and Tripod

1910s Camera

1930s Camera

1940s Press Camera

1950s Camera

1960s Camera

1970s Camera-1 color

1970s Camera-3

1970s Camera-2

1990s Camera

1990s Digital Camera

1970s First filmless electronic camera

Pilot

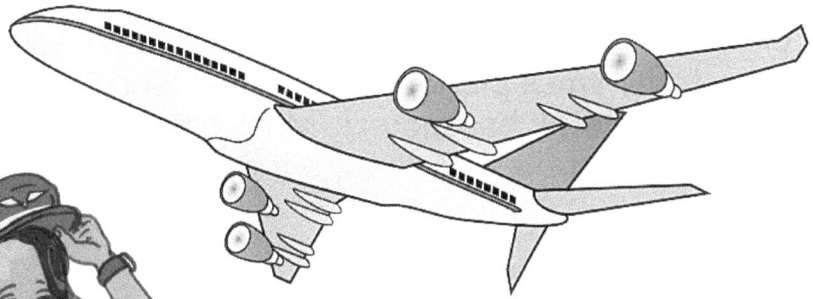

There are more than 2 million pilots in the world. Airline pilots have the opportunity to fly everyday. They must be smart and responsible to keep all the people in the airplane safe.

Pilots wear uniforms and some work for different companies. Some pilots started in the military flying fighter jets and planes.

Pilots for major airlines must obtain the skills to protect people in the air and on the ground. To become a pilot they go to flight school for hundreds of hours. Then, they learn how to use the controls in the cockpit. Learning how to operate any type of airplane is extremely difficult.

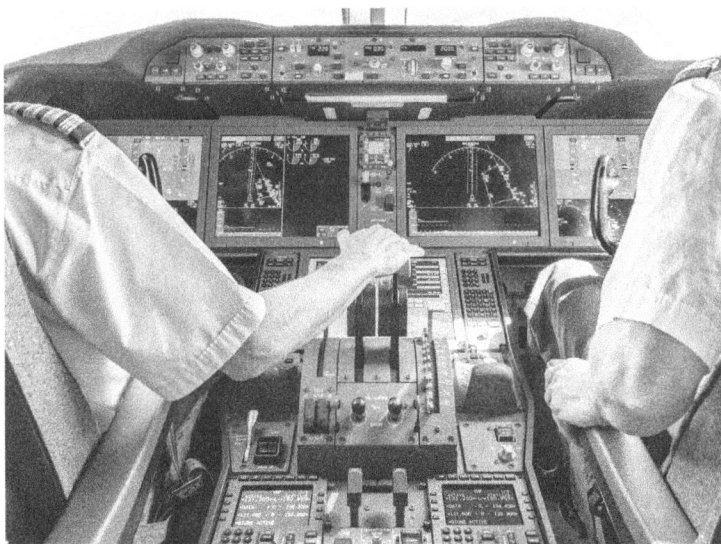

✓ Get your medical certificate.
✓ Get your FAA Student Pilot certificate.
✓ Begin Ground School classes.
✓ Begin flight lessons.
✓ Pass the FAA Private Pilot Knowledge Test.
✓ Pass the FAA Private Pilot Practical Exam.

The next step is to begin your Commercial Pilot training. You must be 18 years old and have a 2nd Class Medical Certificate.

Pilot and copilot in a commercial plane

A pilot's extensive education gives them the ability to fly a wide variety of different types of aircraft. Some of them are taught to fly jumbo jets. Others train to fly small planes. While some learn to fly military planes. Many can also learn to fly helicopters. Most astronauts are pilots and can fly space crafts and shuttles. All require thousands of hours of flight time.

Do you ever dream about being a pilot when you grow up?

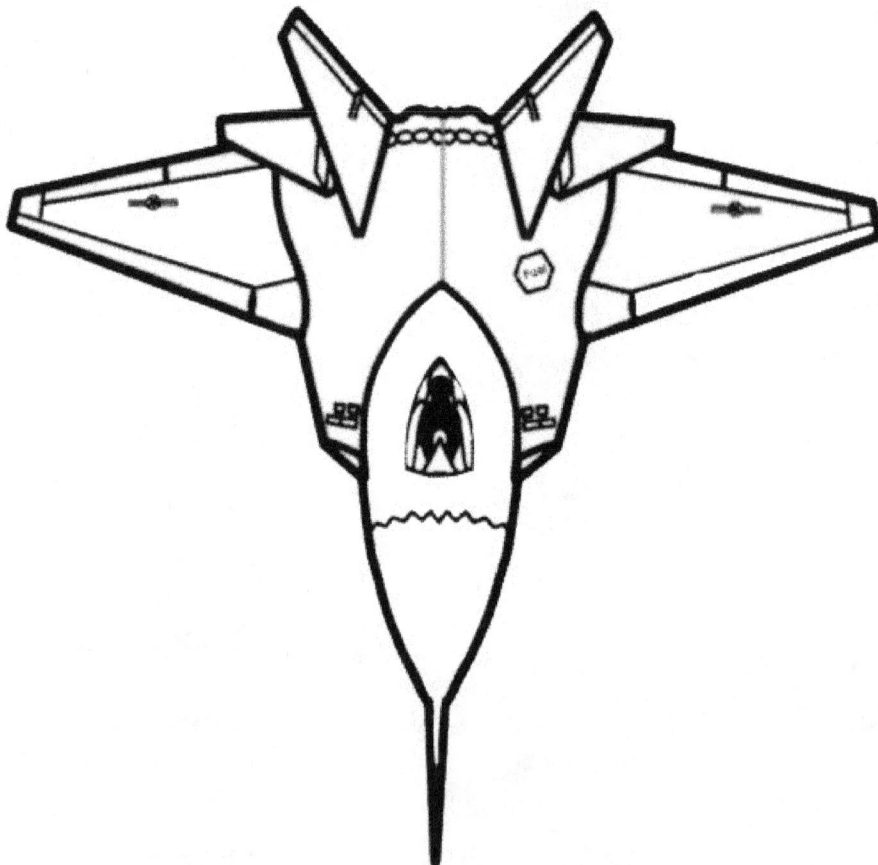

Police

Protect and Serve

baton

LIBERIA NATIONAL POLICE R.L.

police motorcycle

Police officers serve and protect. They also help with crowd control and even deliver important papers from judges.

When a crime happens or there is a problem, do you call the police? Police officers solve more problems than just crime. The police ensure that everyone is constantly protected. They help keep people out of places they should not be at. Police officer help people who are in car accidents. They direct vehicles when traffic lights are out of order. They also evacuate citizens when there are threats like dangerous storms. Police officer make sure people are always safe. Imagine all the problems we would have if there were not any police officer around.

All officers of the law have to go through a lot of police training. First of all, they need to have graduated high school. Some go to college to become an officer. After they finish college, they go to a police academy for training. There, they learn different police tactics. While they are there they learn how to work with civilians. Police officers continue to train throughout their career.

Leadership Characters

Common sense	use good judgment and make wise choices.
Compassion	show understanding and care about others.
Cooperation	work well with others to achieve goals.
Courage	choose to do the right thing even when it is difficult.
Dependable	be trusted to do what is needed.
Diligence	don't give up when the work is hard.
Effort	try your absolute best.
Gratitude	appreciate and thank others.
Initiative	take care of what needs to be done.
Integrity	be honest and fair; always do what is right.
Motivation	work hard to reach goals.
Patience	wait calmly without becoming upset.
Perseverance	keep trying even when trying feels hard.
Pride	be proud of your work and efforts.
Reliable	can be counted on to do what is expected.
Respect	treat others fairly and care about their feelings and needs.
Responsible	be trusted to make the right decisions and do what is expected.
Self-control	control your actions and feelings.
Tolerance	accept others just the way they are.
Trust	be counted on to do what is right.

Elected Politicians

Senator | Representative | Superintendent

A good leader
- ✓ is honest
- ✓ is fair
- ✓ listens
- ✓ encourages
- ✓ doesn't give up
- ✓ show kindness
- ✓ is respectful
- ✓ helps other
- ✓ looks for solutions
- ✓ stays positive

Some government leaders make the rules and laws for the community. Good leaders help their community build schools, hospitals and streets. They also hire people to work and help others in the community.

The national government is made up of an elected president and other elected leaders from around the country. They work together to make the rules and laws for our country.

Seated in the highest office of most countries is the president. The president is the leader of our country, our national government and our military. One of the president's obligations is to engage with leaders from different countries around the world for diplomatic reasons. During his/her time in office, the president can visit many places.

President

The president has lots of responsibilities to the country. He or she helps guide the country with other branches of government. The president gives speeches. He or she is also known as Commander in Chief.

At the time of their inauguration, each president is required under the Constitution to take a presidential oath promising to preserve and defend the Constitution and faithfully execute the law. The oath is administered by the chief justice of Liberia in front of a joint session of the legislature.

So You Want to Be President?

Professional Athletes

Professional athletes play sports for a living. They receive payment for their performance because they have achieved top standing in their chosen sport through years of training. Professional athletes are people with natural talent, stamina, and competitive drive. Those who play team sports may join teams within organized professional leagues. Those who compete in individual sports, such as track or swimming, may make money from sponsorships, corporate endorsements or by winning major events.

Professional Athletes Requirements
✓ Education - High school diploma
✓ Key Skills - Athleticism, concentration, decision-making skills, stamina
✓ Licensure - Licensure or certification is required for some sports and in some localities.

AMERICAN FOOTBALL
ATHLETE
AUTOGRAPH
BASEBALL
BASKETBALL
BOXING
COACHES
COMPETITION
CRICKET
EDUCATION
ENDURANCE
EQUIPMENT
EXERCISE
FIELD HOCKEY
FITNESS

FLEXIBILITY
GOLF
HOCKEY
IN SHAPE
LEAGUES
OFFICIAL
PATIENCE
PENALTIES
PERSEVERANCE
PLAY
POPULAR
POTENTIAL
PROFESSIONAL
QUICKNESS
REFEREE

Let's Play Ball!

RUGBY
SALARY
SOCCER
SOFTBALL
SPORTING EVENTS
SPORTS
STARTING ROSTER
STRENGTH
SWIMMING
TABLE TENNIS
TEAMS
TEAMWORK
TENNIS

TRACK AND FIELD
TRAINING
UMPIRE
UNIQUE SKILLS
VOLLEYBALL
WELLNESS
WORLD CUP
WRESTLING

```
N Y D X Y W D Z E K S M A E T S B G P U C D L R O W
W R E S T L I N G Q X V T Y W K V Z Z P R R L Y N Y
W L S P O R T S S L U M K I M M Z R F A H N E F E J
Q S S E N T I F P T Z I M T L V T K L N O K I T N T
P O T E N T I A L L N M P M F R L U L I C E E B R L
S K L T R H U F P T I E J M U R P Z T O L L O A T A
T K L A T K N T C N K R V G E O T A H D H X I Z D N
A O A B C K I E G K W B B E P N C Q H T I N P K L O
R F B L G B Q K D J M Y P W G U T O A N I Z J P E I
T F T E F K U C M B J H E V D N C L G N M Q L N I S
I I O T L R E I C A L K X E R K I M G P R Y N R F S
N C O E R O S R F S N L E Q E A U T O G R A P H D E
G I F N E W K C M K Z P R Y Y C J P R X L T K N N F
R A N N F M I M T E A N C Q T C N N L O M P Q R A O
O L A I E A L K L T W L I D U T R A R E P G M K K R
S P C S R E L L I B L W S N Y I B E R C A S R K C P
T D I N E T S E W A S B E C O T C S C E M G Z T A F
E L R T E T N N B L X S A L T I I K T C V R U X R M
R H E M Y C R T M L Q R E S L E T L N R O E L E T H
Y F M M E J F S E I T L A N E P N I I E E S S J S E
N L A J J O D L J W Z K V Q L B Y N T B S N R R R F
Z O Y H S B V O L L E Y B A L L A G I E I S G I E Q
Q G V H Y R A L A S M L F Q R Y E L J S P X P T R P
P E N D U R A N C E Z K T P T A M W L Q H M E N H D
B V T I N S H A P E B H K K Y L T Q C T U N O L Q W
N K Y N S E H C A O C C Z T R P N X W X R W N C F T
```

Reporter / Journalist

How do you think it would feel to miss a birthday party because no one told you? There are boatloads of information that needs to be shared. People need to know about the news. A journalist can report about things that happen all over the world. They deliver important information to the public. A journalist can write or report on the news. They share information about what's happening.

Journalists on the TV news or work for magazines and papers are also called reporters. Some interview people.

Journalists have been around for a long time. The first ones used pencils and paper. Later on they also used typewriters. Many of them worked for newspaper or magazine companies. Today, they report information on television news programs and electronically. Can you imagine how it would be to only get information from newspapers?

These days journalists have many ways to report the news. Reporting happens much faster because of technology. It has caused people to use of smart phones and computers to learn information. Due to this, people read blogs, websites, and use apps to learn about the news. Technology is one of the reasons a journalist can share more information on a daily basis.

A news anchorman or anchorwoman is a person who presents news during a news program on TV. News reporting involves discovering all relevant facts, selecting and presenting the important facts and writing an easy-to-understand story.

The purpose of news reporting is to inform people of what is happening in the world around them.

Like any other news journalist/reporters, broadcast reporters research and write stories. Broadcast journalism also requires a sound technician who is responsible for all sound recorded. Interviews are always recorded or filmed and rather than writing a print story, a reporter writes a script for a news package.

reporting the news

What Reporters do:
✓ Keeps up on current events
✓ Travels to different news locations
✓ Gathers information about important events
✓ Has good communicating skills
✓ Conducts interviews
✓ Reports news stories
✓ Works in and out of television studios and radio stations

Robot/Robotics Engineer

A robot can be defined as a machine operated by computer programs that can perform small actions. They can be programmed to do various things. The field in which we study robots is known as Robotics. A robotics engineer is the person responsible for creating and designing robots and robotic systems.

Mostly robots are used to do jobs that involve repetitive actions or dangerous jobs that cannot be done by humans. Robots are also used in military tactics, medicine, to explore other planets or underwater life. A robot is not able to think or make decisions. Electronic sensors are used in the eyes and ears of a robot so that they can sense and process the information about their surroundings. It is only a programmed machine that helps us to get things done.

5 Great Jobs in the Field of Robotics

Robotics Engineer

A robotics engineer is the person responsible for creating and designing robots and robotic systems. He may also be responsible for designing the machines and processes necessary to assemble the robots.

Robotics Technician

A robotics technician has duties similar to a robotics engineer, but this individual will be more focused on testing and repairing robotics systems while helping robotics engineers create and design them. Since she would then be thoroughly knowledgeable about the robotics systems that she worked on, she would spend quite a bit of time working with the customers to ensure that the robots are working properly, usually serving as the liaison between the customers and the robotics engineers.

Sales Engineer

Although these individuals are more focused on the sales aspect of robots and robotic products, they need to be exceptionally knowledgeable about them in order to communicate what ways they will benefit those they are selling to. Sales engineers also need to know how to make adjustments to their merchandise to ensure that it meets the expectations made of it. Individuals with this type of robotics job tend to travel quite a bit with about half of their time spent away from home, depending on what they are selling and to whom.

Software Developer

This individual focuses more on developing the software behind the commands sent to the robotics device. The robot's computer system is pivotal as it essentially provides the brain behind the operation. When a human tells it to do something, whether verbally or by typing in some keystrokes, what the software developer has created inside of it determines how accurately those instructions are carried out. She also ensures that all instructions will be carried out as safely and precisely as possible.

Robotics Operator

Although the idea behind robots and robotics is that they do things that humans cannot do as efficiently, somebody still needs to operate them, whether that involves physically doing something to keep them going or simply overseeing a significant robotics operation to ensure that it continues to operate as intended. Since most robotics are used 24 hours a day, this position would need to be filled by a group of people or by at least having someone on-call on an ongoing basis. If something does go wrong, he would then contact the appropriate robotics salesperson, technician or engineer for assistance if it is not something he can fix himself.

Although some people think that robots are simply taking away jobs, in this case, they are creating them. Also, many believe that allowing robotics to take care of the "dull, dirty and dangerous work" allows people to focus on "creativity and innovation," resulting in an improved world as a result of your job in robotics.

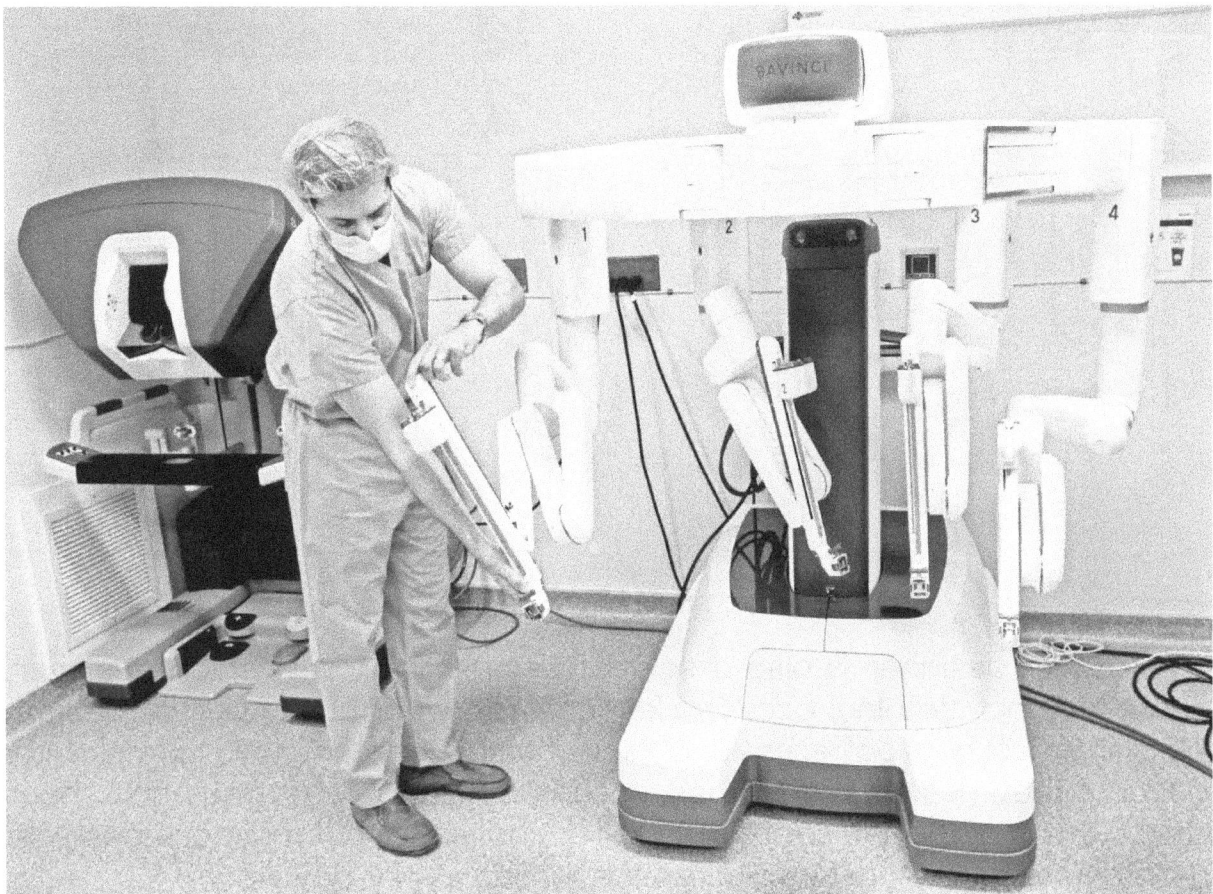

Westerly Hospital robot
The da Vinci Xi Surgical system

This robot will help surgeons with many specific and general surgical procedures.

Seamstress & Taylor (Fashion Designers)

A fashion designer is also a seamstress or a tailor. Fashion designers create original clothing, accessories, and footwear. They sketch designs, select fabrics and patterns, and give instructions on how to make the products they design, like clothes, costume, hats, purses, bags and shoes. Some clothes are made specifically for an individual, but most are designed for the mass market, especially for casual and every-day wear.

Liberian Fashion Designer, Telfar Clemens, designed the 2021 Liberia Olympic team uniforms. Another Liberian Fashion Designer is Korto Momolu, who appeared on Project Runway, an American television show that focuses on fashion design. One day, you could too.

To be a fashion designer, you will need to have a good eye for color and shape. You'll need skills such as pattern-cutting and sewing. Many fashion designers have a bachelor's degree in fashion design. Students learn about textiles and fabrics and how to use computer-aided design (CAD) technology.

Scientist

A scientist is a person who studies or has expertise in science. A scientist tries to understand how our world, or other things, work. Scientists make observations, ask questions and do extensive research work in finding the answers to many questions others may not know about.

What Do Scientists Do?

Scientists observe things. They use their senses when solving science problems. They use their eyes to spot details, they use their noses to detect if something is stinky. They use their hearing, touch, and even sense of taste.

Scientists also measure things. They use scales, rulers, thermometers, and lots of other tools to measure things.

Scientists communicate their findings. They talk about their discoveries and share with others. They tell other scientists or tell other people on the local news or in a book.

Types of Scientist

An archeologist is a scientist who studies how people lived in the past.

An astronomer is a scientist who studies space.

A botanist is a scientist who studies plants.

An environmentalist is a scientist who studies the environment.

A geographer is a scientist who studies Earth's physical features.

An ethologist is a scientist who studies animal behaviors.

A geologist is a scientist who studies rocks.

A marine biologist is a scientist who studies animals that live in the sea.

A meteorologist is a scientist who studies the weather.

A microbiologist is a scientist who studies tiny living things like bacteria and fungi.

A paleontologist is a scientist who studies fossils.

A zoologist is a scientist who studies animals.

You can be a scientist too!
Do you have the characteristics of a good scientist?

✓ Scientists are curious about their world. They want to know why things happen and how things work.

✓ Scientists are patient as they repeat experiments many times to verify results.

✓ Scientists are courageous. They work to discover answers often times for years and with many failures. They recognize that failed experiments provide answers as often as successful ones.

✓ Scientist pay close attention to details. Detailed observations in one experiment could also lead to answers in another.

✓ Scientists must be creative, able to think outside the box and envision things that cannot be seen.
✓ Scientists are persistent. Their work may take decades, and their approach may be wrong, and their work could be proven false by future scientists; but they continue on their experiment.
✓ Scientists need good communication skills. They may need to work as part of a team, share information with the public or work with colleagues around the world.
✓ Scientists need to be open-minded and not judge so they can continue to observe and collect data while searching for the best possible solution.
✓ Careful thinkers and problem-solvers. Scientists need to analyze information and make important decisions to solve experimental problems or world problems.

Find the types of scientist in the puzzle below.

ARCHEOLOGIST
ASTRONOMER
BOTANIST
ENVIRONMENTALIST
ETHOLOGIST
GEOGRAPHER
GEOLOGIST
MARINE BIOLOGIST
METEOROLOGIST
MICROBIOLOGIST
PALEONTOLOGIST
ZOOLOGIST

```
D T J J Y D F P F T R K G T E M
T P S H C K T L F E T E S M N T
N N J I H J M G M T O I E I V S
L T S I G O L O E G G T T C I I
T K G L D O N H R O E R S R R G
T Z H X Q O L A L O P Z I O O O
G E J X R J P O R B H H G B N L
D Z T T P H T O O Q G T O I M O
T K S H E N L M P Z M P L O E I
T A R R O O N K M H L W O L N B
K C W E G L J P P C M T E O T E
J M L I T L O W W D W L H G A N
R A S M R L J G H Z B M C I L I
P T C F L R Z P I T Y L R S I R
N X Z B O T A N I S T F A T S A
L W W K W T R K T L T H L R T M
```

Soldier

✓ Protects our country
✓ Respectful and loyal
✓ Protects our freedom
✓ Performs rescue operations
✓ Has a very dangerous job
✓ Away from home a lot
✓ Wears a special uniform
✓ Must go through a lot of training

Military Member

A soldier is a member of the military. The military, or armed forces, protects a country's land, sea, and airspace from foreign invasion. An army protects the land, the navy protects the sea, and an air force protects the airspace.

Soldiers have one job: to protect their country. However, there are many different ways to do this. If the country is at war, many soldiers fight in combat. They use weapons and technology to help defeat the enemy. During peacetime, soldiers are alert to any danger or threat to their country.

Soldiers who enlist in the military without a college education enter as privates. Soldiers must be at least 18 years old, have a high school diploma, and be in good physical shape.

Teacher

Teachers share information and inspire people to start businesses, write, sing, explore, and live successful lives to help make the world a better place.

What do you think the world would be like without teachers? Things would be much more complicated. Some people may not have very many accomplishments. The reason teachers have an important task is because they inspire people of all ages. They make children want to create things such as cars, buildings, and inventions. A teacher passes on information. Because of their hard work students become artists, engineers, and scientists.

Successful teachers follow a difficult process to earn their diploma. First, teachers go to college. Next, they must pass a professional test. For example, a gym coach must pass the physical education exam and then must get certified. Their certification or licensure must be in the country or state they plan to practice teaching. A teacher in Liberia need to get licensed in Liberia. A teacher in New York would need to get licensed in New York. If they move to another country or state, then they would need to get a certificate from that country or state. Ultimately, successful teachers have a career of twenty to thirty years.

There are many different kinds of teachers. Professional teachers are kindergarten teachers to college professors. In many places, teachers are also called instructors. Likewise, a teacher can be anyone that teaches a skill. These people can be coaches, parents, and trainers. Have you ever taught anyone something new? Perhaps you taught someone to tie their shoes. If so, you were a teacher.

Discover the hidden words in the puzzle. Remember, words run not only vertically, horizontally, and diagonally, but may be spelled backwards as well. If you get stuck, the answers are included at the back of the book.

People We Learn From

COACH
EDUCATOR
GUIDE
INSTRUCTOR
MENTOR
PROFESSOR
SCHOLAR
TEACHER
TRAINER
TUTOR

H	D	W	J	K	Y	R	R	W	I
G	U	I	D	E	Y	O	E	B	N
T	T	M	T	F	T	D	N	S	S
B	P	L	E	A	H	H	I	C	T
L	X	K	C	N	T	C	A	H	R
R	C	U	N	U	T	A	R	O	U
R	D	P	T	Q	J	O	T	L	C
E	H	O	D	V	Q	C	R	A	T
P	R	O	F	E	S	S	O	R	O
L	N	T	E	A	C	H	E	R	R

✓ Enjoys teaching new things
✓ Helps others
✓ Has a lot of patience
✓ Respects everyone
✓ Uses books, pencils, and computers
✓ Works in schools
✓ Cares about their students
✓ Treats everyone equally
✓ Loves learning

Trash Collector/Sanitation Workers

Clean and Sanitary – a trash collector has an important job because garbage is very dangerous. Uncollected garbage causes diseases and sickness. Pests like roaches, rats, and other animals look for food in the trash. Trash collectors are brave because their work is to remove the garbage to keep neighborhoods clean. They work very hard from sunup to sundown and sometimes in the rain.

Just think about how dirty everything was when garbage was not collected? Trash was thrown into the street, and it was not picked up. Managing waste is a great idea because the streets are free of litter. Nowadays, trash collectors use machines to pick up trash and do not have to touch any of it.

Veterinarian or Vet Tech

Most veterinarians diagnose animal health problems, vaccinate animals against diseases, medicate animals suffering from infections or illnesses, treat and dress wounds, set fractures, perform surgery, and advise owners about animal feeding, behavior, and breeding.

✓ Gives animals shots and medicine
✓ Has a lot of patience
✓ Knows a lot about animals
✓ Helps our pets when they are sick
✓ Takes care of animals
✓ Works in an office or a zoo
✓ Cares about all animals
✓ Teach others how to care for animals

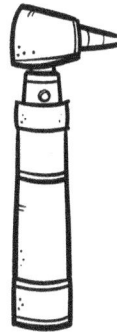

band aid

Vet tech perform duties for animals that are similar to what a nurse might do for humans. They support veterinarians in the diagnostic and treatment of sick and healthy animals.

Do you have a passion for medicine, science, and animals and enjoy working with people, then it's absolutely worth it.

Volunteer

Helping the Community

pick up litter   help an old person   feed a homeless person

Volunteering means spending some of your free time helping others. You may volunteer to help other people, such as the families who lost their homes after a fire. You can also volunteer to protect animals in Sapo National Park, the environment, or any other cause that you care about. To volunteer means to give without being asked and without being paid.

What Great Volunteers Have In Common:
✓ They have a lot of courage.
✓ They need to be patient and stick it out
✓ A good volunteer follow instructions and do them
✓ Identify what needs to be done and start working on it yourself.
✓ Remember you're there to help, not to prove yourself. Stay humble.
✓ Genuine passion for their work, look at the work as something important.
✓ Work as a team, every member brings a special set of skills and is important.

Volunteering is a great way to be a valued member of a community. You meet different people and make new friends. Volunteering feels good, and let you know that you can make a difference.

Volunteering is a great way to be a valued member of your community.

Waiter & Waitress

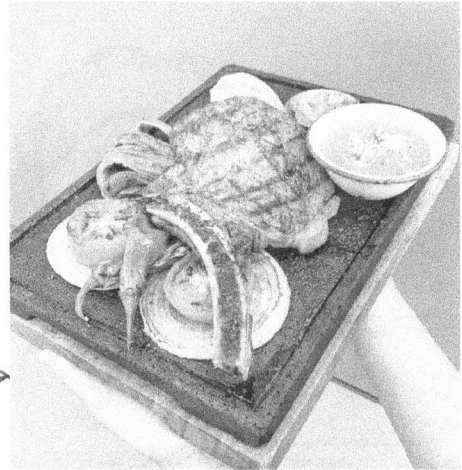

✓ Work well with others
✓ Accept criticism
✓ Pay attention to detail
✓ Willing to help people
✓ Good listening skills
✓ A good memory

A waiter is a person who serves food and drinks to people at tables, often at a restaurant or cafe. A female waiter is called a waitress. They will take orders and deliver food to customers. They play an important role in customer satisfaction because they are also responsible for checking on customers to make sure that they are enjoying their meals. They also take action to correct any problems.

What do waiter and waitress do?

1. Greet customers as they arrive and show them to their table.
2. Give out menus and take orders for food and drinks.
3. Answer questions about menu items and give advice on ingredients.
4. Take food orders to kitchen staff.
5. Serve food and drinks.
6. Make sure customers are happy with their meals and handle any complaints.
7. Clear away used dishes and cutlery from tables.
8. Deal with bill payments
9. Make sure tables are clean and tidy for the next the customers.

Writer/Author

✓ Uses their imagination
✓ Loves to write
✓ Takes chances
✓ Tells a story
✓ Sets goals and deadlines
✓ Writes papers and books
✓ Has patience
✓ Keeps an open mind

WRITING PROCESS

PRE-WRITING
DRAFTING
WRITING
REVISING
EDITING
PROOF READING
PUBLISHING

The main job of a writer is to write meaningful stories which can teach, educate and inform people. Writers create material for many different things such as books, magazines, newspapers, television and advertising. They write fiction or nonfiction. Writers often have editors who review their work. Editors are often writers too.

Some writers work for businesses, but many work on their own. Writing can be a very satisfying job. Writers can write about any topic which is interesting to them. A college degree is required for a position as a writer. Most employers prefer to hire people with degrees in communications, journalism, or English.

A writer develops original written content for mediums such as advertisements, books, magazines, movies, and television scripts. They also create new ideas for the subject or topic that is part of a book.

Zookeeper

Zookeepers are the basic caregivers for animals in a zoo. They take care of zoo animals that are kept in captivity for conservation or to be displayed to the public. He or she is usually responsible for daily feeding and caring for the animals. As part of their routine, they may clean the exhibits and report health problems. Zookeepers may also be involved in science research or public education, such as conducting tours and answering questions.

Zookeeper Skills

✓ Understand animal behavior.
✓ Know care techniques and how to handle animals.
✓ Experience with common grooming techniques, including caring for coats, cleaning ears and clipping nails.
✓ Able to lift heavy objects, bending and kneeling.

A zookeeper typically has a degree in an animal-related field such as animal science, biology, or zoology.

Entrepreneur

Successful Entrepreneur

Adenah Bayoh

After escaping civil war in Liberia, Adenah Bayoh opened her first IHOP (International House of Pancakes) at age 26 and now owns four in and around Newark, N.J. — plus three other restaurants.

An entrepreneur is someone who builds businesses to make money. Entrepreneurs are often creative, daring people, and the businesses they operate are very important to communities.

Entrepreneur make money 1 in 4 ways:
They buy and sell
They buy and rent
They ccreate and sell
They create and rent

Where do great ideas for a new business come from? Entrepreneurs are constantly coming up with new ideas that they turn into new businesses.

Some of the best products and services in the world come from creating a solution for a problem and making people's life easier.

So you want to be an entrepreneur? Start your own business.

Become a Spa Business Owner

The Pampering People Spa

candles

hot stones

massage

manicure

foot bath

sticks diffuser

hairdryer

spa shoes

robe

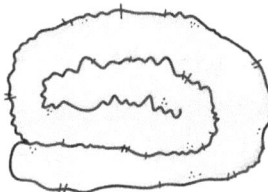

towel folded

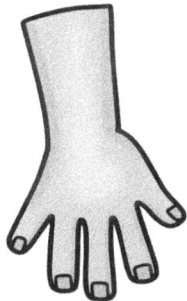

polished
nails

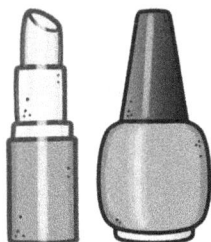

sauna

More Jobs, Careers & Occupations

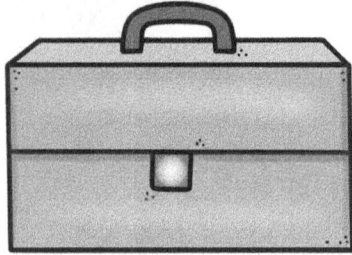

tool box

Coach

Electrician

✓ CHALLENGES THEIR TEAM
✓ KNOWS A LOT ABOUT SPORTS
✓ INSPIRES THEIR TEAM
✓ SHARES THEIR PASSION FOR SPORTS
✓ ENCOURAGES EVERYONE
✓ TEACHES ABOUT THE IMPORTANCE OF TEAMWORK
✓ MAKES SPORTS FUN FOR EVERYONE
✓ SHOWS THAT THEY ARE PATIENT

✓ FIXES THINGS LIKE TELEVISIONS, FANS AND LIGHTS
✓ WORKS WITH ELECTRICITY
✓ RESPONSIBLE AND CAREFUL
✓ MAKES SURE BUILDINGS ARE SAFE
✓ WORKS INDOORS AND OUTDOORS
✓ WORKS WITH SCREWDRIVERS, WIRES, AND LIGHT BULBS
✓ TAKES THEIR TIME
✓ KNOWS A LOT ABOUT ELECTRICITY

Gardener

✓ KNOWS A LOT ABOUT PLANTS AND FLOWERS
✓ MAKES OUR COMMUNITY LOOK NICE
✓ USES TOOLS, SUCH AS WATERING CANS AND SHOVELS
✓ CARES ABOUT THE ENVIRONMENT
✓ TAKES CARE OF PLANTS
✓ KEEPS GARDENS HEALTHY

Janitor

✓ WORKS IN SCHOOLS AND OTHER BUILDINGS
✓ USES TOOLS, SUCH AS BUCKETS AND MOPS
✓ KEEPS RESTROOMS CLEAN
✓ CLEANS SPILLS AND OTHER MESSES
✓ KEEPS PLACES CLEAN AND SAFE
✓ ENJOYS CLEANING
✓ EMPTIES THE TRASH

Librarian

✓ ORGANIZE AND FRIENDLY
✓ LIKES TO HELP PEOPLE
✓ TAKES CARE OF THE LIBRARY
✓ KNOWS A LOT ABOUT BOOKS
✓ HELPS PEOPLE FIND INFORMATION
✓ HELPS PEOPLE FIND BOOKS
✓ TEACHES CHILDREN
✓ LIKES TO READ
✓ WORKS IN A SCHOOL OR LIBRARY

METEOROLOGIST

✓ STUDIES AND PREDICTS THE WEATHER
✓ USES RADARS, SATELLITES, AND WEATHER STATIONS
✓ INFORMS THE PUBLIC ABOUT DANGEROUS WEATHER
✓ HELPS KEEP US SAFE
✓ MONITORS WEATHER CONDITIONS
✓ HELPS US DECIDE WHAT TO WEAR
✓ KNOWS A LOT ABOUT CLIMATE AND THE ENVIRONMENT

PARAMEDIC

✓ DRIVES AN AMBULANCE
✓ CARES FOR SICK AND INJURED PEOPLE
✓ COMMUNICATES WITH DOCTORS
✓ TRANSPORTS PEOPLE TO HOSPITALS
✓ RESPONDS TO EMERGENCY CALLS
✓ TREATS WOUNDS
✓ PROVIDES MEDICAL TREATMENT
✓ GIVES MEDICATIONS
✓ ENJOYS TAKING CARE OF PEOPLE

PRINCIPAL

✓ WORKS IN SCHOOLS
✓ EVALUATES TEACHERS
✓ DISCIPLINES STUDENTS
✓ CARES ABOUT ALL STUDENTS
✓ STAYS INVOLVED WITH STUDENTS, PARENTS AND THE COMMUNITY
✓ POSITIVE AND ENTHUSIASTIC
✓ HELPS STUDENTS LEARN
✓ ENJOYS HELPING OTHERS
✓ IS A GOOD LEADER

SECRETARY

- ✓ FILES IMPORTANT PAPERS
- ✓ ANSWERS PHONE CALLS
- ✓ TYPES LETTERS AND EMAILS
- ✓ SCHEDULES APPOINTMENTS
- ✓ KEEPS RECORDS
- ✓ KEEPS EVERYONE ORGANIZED
- ✓ HAS A FRIENDLY ATTITUDE
- ✓ KEEPS TRACK OF SCHEDULES
- ✓ WORKS IN AN OFFICE OR SCHOOL

MAIL CARRIER

- ✓ WEARS A BLUE UNIFORM
- ✓ HELPS US STAY CONNECTED
- ✓ STAYS ORGANIZED
- ✓ WORKS OUTSIDE, EVEN IN THE RAIN AND SNOW
- ✓ MAKES SURE YOUR MAIL GETS TO THE RIGHT PLACE
- ✓ DELIVERS LETTERS AND PACKAGES
- ✓ WALKS OR DRIVES A MAIL TRUCK

Growth Mindset vs Fixed Mindset Challenge

Read each statement. Circle whether the statement represents a growth mindset or a fixed mindset.

I like challenging myself because it helps me to gain new knowledge.	
Growth Mindset	Fixed Mindset

If I make a mistake, I will not achieve my goal.	
Growth Mindset	Fixed Mindset

The more I practice kicking, the better I will be at scoring goals.	
Growth Mindset	Fixed Mindset

I tried to work this problem out, but I just can't get the right answer.	
Growth Mindset	Fixed Mindset

I don't know what to write about because I'm not creative.	
Growth Mindset	Fixed Mindset

If I set a goal, I can achieve it, even if it takes some time.	
Growth Mindset	Fixed Mindset

My parents can't read well, so that's why I can't read well.	
Growth Mindset	Fixed Mindset

In order to be successful, I must first experience failure.	
Growth Mindset	Fixed Mindset

If I work hard and do my best, it doesn't matter if I win or lose.	
Growth Mindset	Fixed Mindset

I will never be as smart as that kid.	
Growth Mindset	Fixed Mindset

I don't understand fractions because I'm not good at math.	
Growth Mindset	Fixed Mindset

I'm having trouble playing the drums, so I am going to switch to a new instrument.	
Growth Mindset	Fixed Mindset

So Many Jobs, Careers & Occupations A-L
when I grow up, I want to be a . . .

Accountant
Animal Trainer
Architect
Artist
Astronaut
Astronomer
Athlete
Author
Baker
Banker
Baseball Player
Basketball Player

Builder
Bus Driver
Business Man
Business Woman
Cashier
Chef
Coach
Computer Engineer
Construction worker
Dancer
Delivery Person
Dentist

Detective
Diamond Miner
Doctor
Farmer
Fashion Designer
Firefighter
Fisherman
Florist
Football Player
Garbage
Collector
Gardener

Hairstylist
Hockey Player
Janitor
Judge
Lawyer
Librarian
Lifeguard
Magician
Mail Carrier

```
R J K K D R A U G E F I L X L R M V L V D O C T O R W
C O A A R C H I T E C T M D T F R M F Z M L W B N R P
H O H N B Z V V K H E T E L H T A E R L Q D M Y R R C
V F N T I Y R Q M R T L L V R G F E I M Y R K E G W Q
F N L S U T K M Z R N N G E M C N L F H M W N D Y Y F
G L V H T A O X R B J T K V G I L I N J S I K A C L L
K J H H C R K R N Q T N Z R A C R N K R M A Y N K J K
X B R H T E U Q X K A V K R D E M B W D K S C C L J H
X A E T Y K R C F B G T T Q F R V T N R F T N E N C T
T S V L K A J L T J W L B I N B Z O J N R R K R A F J
R K I T B B L T U I A R G T U Q M F D F F O N O I G F
F E T W S L W D T M O H E S B A F E L G J N C M R A E
A T C T M I G C I S T N D Y I Q L A X A W A R Z A R H
S B E M T E T N H E I R W D W I K N R K R U R T R B C
H A T R N C A N R T I R K O V A T R B M P T F J B A P
I L E R A K K C E V F P O E R T L G B V E T I J I G M
O L D E T C L Z E D L L R L S K M Y K U M R M S L E Y
N P K N N R M R X Y R Y A I F Y E H M N I T L P T C L
D L N E U R T R M N P S L Y N P Y R M K W L Z P V O L
E A K D O Y X D V E T Y H K Y M V M V M D T D X T L W
S Y R R C L D K R R T B A S E B A L L P L A Y E R L L
I E T A C K C S O S C T H H O C K E Y P L A Y E R E K
G R D G A K O N R Z H N A M O W S S E N I S U B V C W
N T V R W N O I C O M P U T E R E N G I N E E R T T K
E B T Y H M A M J J J N A M R E H S I F V J J K Y O G
R J C T E H R E Y A L P L L A B T O O F N K R G T R C
V N B R R L N K T C M F Z N A M S S E N I S U B L C L
```

So Many Jobs, Careers & Occupations M-Z

Make-Up Artist
Market-woman
Mayor
Mechanic
Meteorologist
Miner
Model
Movie Star
Musician
Nail Artist
Nanny
News Reporter
Nurse
Office worker

Olympian
Painter
Paleontologist
Paramedic
Pastor
Pharmacist
Photographer
Pilot
Plumber
Police Officer
President
Principal
Psychologist
Race Car Driver

Radio Host
Radiologist
Rock Star
Sales man
Sales woman
Scientist
Scuba Diver
Secretary
Skater
Soccer Player
Soldier
Taxi Driver
Teacher
Tour Guide

Trainer
Veterinarian
Waiter
Waitress
Weather Reporter
Writer
Zoo Keeper

```
B N A I R A N I R E T E V V D R E H P A R G O T O H P C V
P F R M E L W N Z P A L E O N T O L O G I S T R H M L K T
F K Q X I G B A P R L M T N R J V D S A L E S W O M A N R
R K P J D R X I D T T K A E A H Q Y W C H R T T M N R E B
L S G L L L K C N M W R C R H I D B H F A Y K K E W T W P
G F S X O M G I L C K I E B K W L F H T P G G W R I A T A
H R Q E S B R G P C F N P K V E T A S K T Y S G R I R S S
Y K A P R E G A W F L H S N R P T E R L L R B W T E T C T
R R N T T T Y M O J A T Y H N O I - J T E L X E V T T U O
P V R N S K I E K R N R C F X V W X W P I G R I B C X B R
R H I E J K C A M Z A X H L O D H E O O D S R L H B P A F
X A N Y Y I C A W D W D O M Q M K R C R M D T L N D B D R
P M A T L A C O I W M N L N G D T R T I R A S E A K K I E
G A I O O I L O R R L G O P V E R R K A F E N D N V L V T
N Y P P S L H P E L R D G P R L E G C M C F B O N L T E R
C O M T R O I V R F Z R I R A I X E M R L R O M Y N F R O
V R Y R S I I P M E L N S T R R C D E N K K R K J A T J P
J V L T S R N E T C C G T R L A A T T K R M J L L M C C E
D M O K D C C C K N Q C A N R V A M L O M E L K T S H B R
Z N Z I K H I Q I K M C O T M R K M E K U L N W N E R N R
L R X D A C Y E T P L Q T S Y T H V H D D R L I R L T K E
M A W N N C Q M N I A Y R E T A K S C D I C G P M A J N H
T K I R M N T Z A T M L Z D P B N M J W N C M U M S H R T
R C B E V K W M T S I G O L O R O E T E M F J C I L P L A
A H Z B L Y W G F L D S Z K B G P R E S I D E N T D M B E
I D P M B T V L D H Q K T L C T C E S R U N W Q K H E N W
N T G U Q K R B T E A C H E R K H L Z R P M U S I C I A N
E K L L M A K E - U P A R T I S T Z O O K E E P E R X N X
R D N P N G B C N R F V W R B C T S I G O L O I D A R N D
```

Low Paying Jobs

Find the low paying jobs in the puzzle.

ANIMAL CARETAKER (NON-FARM ANIMALS)
BABYSITTER
BARTENDER
CASHIER
COOK
DESK CLERK
DISHWASHER
DRY CLEANER
FARMHAND
FAST FOOD COOK
FOOD PREP
FOOD SERVER

GAMBLING DEALER
HAND PACKER
HOUSEKEEPER
KITCHEN HELPER
MAID
MANICURIST
PARKING LOT ATTENDANT
PEDICURIST
PERSONAL CARE AIDE
SHAMPOOER
TICKET TAKER
USHER

WAITER (SERVER)
WAITRESS (SERVER)

```
M D K V N V R L C D L X W K R M T D M K L T P
Z H V R W X P E E A S X L G W M H V O P G W E
G D P F J L F S P S S L C N R A K O K R W G R
G L Z E G Q K O E L F H S B N E C V N M Y F S
A F L F D C L R O N E H I D Z D H K R L Y R O
M Z F L L I T Y M D A H P E O J J S Q J X E N
B L R E J I C R F M S A N O R Q Q Q U T N K A
L T R C A K M U P Q C E F E M X V K X P R A L
I K V W K P W O R K R T R V H G D T B F D T C
N K M H F N O V E I S B T V G C D L G T D E A
G T K C N E R R N A S V Z K E G T T R F C R R
D T R L R X P T F D C T X X G R S I R C X A E
E H T C J R E H S A W H S I D I X E K R K C A
A W W L B F P Z D R T T V R R M T R P E R L I
L B A R T E N D E R E T Z U N T C T D T M A D
E T F W C Q N G V F N N C N I G O V N I V M E
R E K A T T E K C I T I A S M R O R A A K I D
D T V W H V T F X X N R Y E H W K B H W B N T
F O O D P R E P P A R B M R L F M T M H K A Q
M D N V Y L H B M L A H V V X C M R R K K G D
L I H H Y N G H Z B F V G K Z M Y L A R R T K
Z A C L N C R E P E E K E S U O H R F P L Y T
C M W P A R K I N G L O T A T T E N D A N T K
```

High Paying Jobs

Find the high paying jobs in the puzzle.

ACCOUNTANT
AIRLINE PILOT
ANESTHESIOLOGIST
CEO (Chief executive officer)
DENTIST
DOCTOR
ENGINEER
IT manager (short for Information Technology)

LAW TEACHER
LAWYER
MARKETING MANAGER
NEUROSURGEON
OBSTETRICIAN
ORTHODONTIST
PEDIATRICIAN
PODIATRIST
PSYCHIATRIST
SURGEON

```
Q  N  M  A  R  K  E  T  I  N  G  M  A  N  A  G  E  R
Q  A  N  E  S  T  H  E  S  I  O  L  O  G  I  S  T  F
L  B  Z  D  M  Y  N  T  V  Q  N  X  R  Q  Q  F  R  R
J  T  O  E  W  X  N  L  S  F  T  E  T  P  N  K  L  E
N  S  B  N  R  C  M  E  J  I  Y  J  E  M  T  R  Q  H
N  I  S  T  M  L  M  G  U  W  R  D  W  O  W  D  G  C
T  R  T  I  B  R  Y  X  A  R  I  T  L  C  T  M  D  A
T  T  E  S  M  X  L  L  D  A  O  I  A  Y  T  T  H  E
N  A  T  T  D  M  M  O  T  R  P  S  N  I  H  X  T  T
A  I  R  G  G  W  C  R  M  E  E  L  U  V  D  W  B  W
T  H  I  Y  N  T  I  R  N  M  R  G  Q  R  N  O  D  A
N  C  C  N  O  C  N  I  G  C  R  P  A  M  G  B  P  L
U  Y  I  R  I  O  L  N  J  K  E  V  T  N  T  E  F  C
O  S  A  A  E  R  L  X  V  L  C  O  L  T  A  B  O  V
C  P  N  G  I  L  R  L  G  F  T  R  T  N  L  M  Q  N
C  W  R  A  L  P  V  P  B  P  R  J  Q  D  J  V  T  W
A  U  T  S  I  T  N  O  D  O  H  T  R  O  B  N  Q  I
S  Y  W  R  E  E  N  I  G  N  E  T  L  F  R  P  J  V
```

*A chief executive officer, is the highest-ranking person in a company or institution. He/she is responsible for making managerial decisions.

**A marketing manager's job is to promote a business, product, or service. They make sure that the company is communicating the right messaging to attract future customers and retain existing ones.

Getting the Job

Buying items like food, drink, toys and clothes cost money. When you're old enough, you can get a job to earn some money for yourself. To get a job, you should look for job adverts online, in stores or in newspapers.

Job seekers read classifieds

You can ask your family or career advisor in school to help you. When you apply for a job, you have to give them a resume about yourself. You can have help to write this.

The company may call me for an interview if they like my cv.

For the job interview, you should dress smart and arrive early. In the interview, you will be asked lots of questions. Answer these as best as you can. You should smile, be confident, kind and keep good eye contact as well as being polite. You should smile, be confident, kind and keep good eye contact as well as being polite. When the interview is over, you shall thank them and then leave. If you get the job, they will phone and let you know. If you do not get the job, it is ok, you can apply for another job. They might have had lots of people applying for one job.

Presenting your skills, talents, and experience to potential employers, whether in writing or in person, is a key part of getting any job.

Applying for a Job - Whether responding to an advertised job or meeting with an employer in person, take time to think about your job application.

1. Research - Use the internet or use other means by asking people who know about the employer, and do some research, into your potential employer. What do they do? What makes them distinctive? What is happening in their sector of the market?
2. Read the job description: Make sure you read the job description very carefully. Employers usually specify skills and qualifications that are essential to the job, so make sure your application indicates that you meet the specific job requirements.
3. Fine-Tune your CV: Don't send out the same, standard resume or CV to all potential employers. Think about what each employer is looking for, and try to include evidence of success in these specific areas.
4. Choose your words: think carefully about the words you use to describe your skills and achievements. Try to compare the language used in the job description or on the company website.

Getting Through The Interview - If an employer is impressed by your application, you may be invited to attend an interview.

1. Prepare and Relax: make sure you prepare thoroughly for the interview. Remember that it is natural to feel nervous beforehand, so try to find ways to relax. You could play music or do some breathing exercises.
2. Dress for success: you should always be well dressed for an interview. This does not always mean wearing a suit; try to match the style of dress within the organization.
3. Know yourself: make sure you review your resume or CV before you attend the interview. Be clear about the skills and qualifications you have to offer the employer. Think of examples of your past achievements in advance.
4. Have answers to standard questions: prepare answers for some of the most common interview questions, such as; "Tell me about yourself." "Why are you interested in this role?" "Why do you think you are the right person for this job?"

Job Vocabulary

401K: this is an account that helps people with retirement (in the US)

Apprenticeship: a hands-on job training program.

Benefits: these are good things that your employee might help pay for.

Company: an association of persons operating a business.

Compensation: how much you get paid.

Cover Letter: a 3-4 paragraph letter that tells the employer more about you.

Deductions: this is the amount of money taken out from your paycheck.

Direct Deposit: to have your paycheck deposited directly into your account.

Employee: a person working for a company.

Employer: a person or company that hires you.

Entry-Level: a job that requires little to no experience.

Full-time: usually, this means working 40 hours a week.

Gross Pay: this is how much money you make before taxes (in the US)

Hourly Pay: this is how much money you make every hour you work.

Insurance: you can pay for insurance for things like life, dental, and medical.

Interview: a meeting with a future employer to try and get a job.

IRS: the part of the government that is responsible for tax-related topics (in the US)

Minimum Wage: this is the lowest amount you can get paid per hour legal in your state (in the US)

Net Pay: this is how much money you actually bring home after taxes are taken out.

Occupation: a job or career someone has.

Overtime: this is when you work more than your usual hours.

Part-time: working only a part of the day or week (ex: 10 hours a week)

Pay Stub: a piece of paper that shows how much you earned and how much you paid in taxes.

Personal Leave: this is time you can take off for your own personal reasons.

Position: the specific type of job you might be doing (ex: cashier)

Promotion: to move up within the company.

Qualifications: a quality that an employer is looking for to make sure you are a good fit for the job.

Reference: these are people who your employer can call to learn about your work experience

Resume: a document that summarizes and skills.

Salary: this is the fixed amount of money your make every month or year.

Seasonal Worker: a person who only works on specific months of the year.

Sick Leave: this is time you can take off because of medical reasons

Strengths: something that you are good at.

Supervisor: a manager or someone

responsible for their employees.

Timesheet: a piece of paper that shows how many hours you worked.

Unemployed: this means you currently do not have a job.

Union Dues: this is what you pay to be a part of the union at work.

Vacancy: a job opening.

W2: this is a form sent by your employer showing how much you made and paid in taxes for the year. (in the US)

W4: this is the form that helps your employer know how much taxes to hold from your paycheck (in the US)

Weaknesses: something that you are bad at.

If I get the job, I will probably have to wear a uniform like everyone else. I should arrive early for my job each day and work to the best of my ability. Each month I will get paid from my job, some of my money will go on taxes.

Having a job will mean I can make money to buy things that I want. It also means that I am growing up and becoming an independent adult.

Answers

P. 20 Change Your Mindset

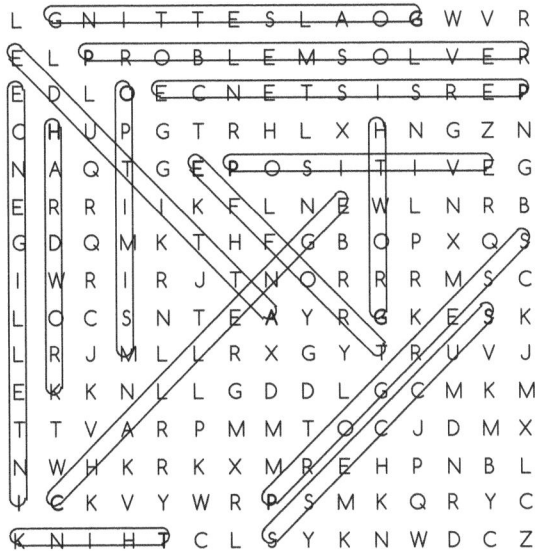

```
L G N I T T E S L A O G W V R
E L P R O B L E M S O L V E R
E D L O E C N E T S I S R E P
C H U P G T R H L X H N G Z N
N A Q T G E P O S I T I V E G
E R R I K F L N E W L N R B
G D Q M K T H F G B O P X Q S
I W R I R J T N O R R M S C
L O C S N T E A Y R C K E S K
L R J M L L R X G Y J R U V K
E K N L L G D D L G C M K M
T V A R P M M T O C J D M X
N W H K R K X M R E H P N B L
C K V Y W R P S M K Q R Y C
K N I H T C L S Y K N W D C Z
```

P. 26 Applying for College

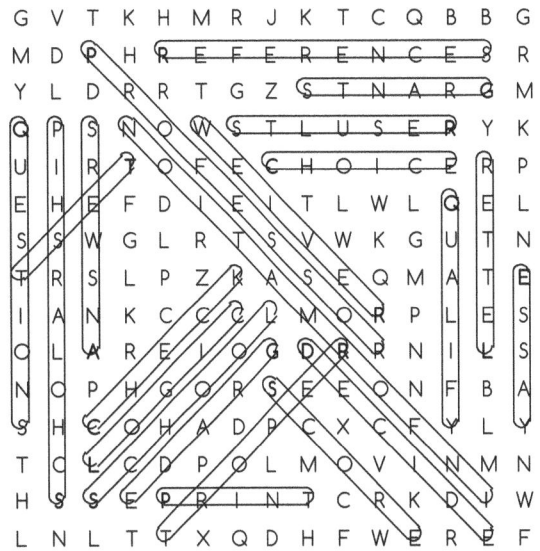

```
G V T K H M R J K T C Q B B G
M D P H R E F E R E N C E S R
Y L D R R T G Z S T N A R G M
Q P S N O W S T L U S E R Y K
U I R T O F E C H O I C E P
E H E F D I E I T L W L G E L
S S W G L R T S V W K G U T N
T A L K C C L M O R P L E S
I N O P H G O R S E E O N F B A
O N C O H A D P C X C F L Y
N L C D P O L M O V I N M N
T H S E P R I N T C R K D J W
L N L T T X Q D H F W E R E F
```

P. 54 Farm Tools & Equipments

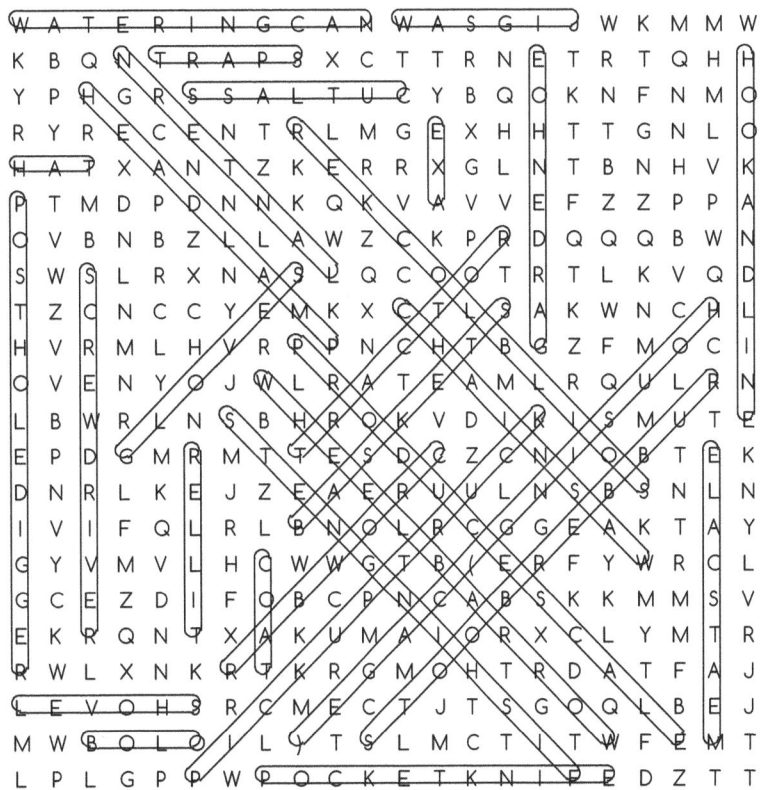

```
W A T E R I N G C A N W A S G I W K M M W
K B Q H T R A P S X C T T R N E T R T Q H
Y P H G R S S A L T U C Y B Q O K N F N M O
R Y R E C E N T R L M G E X H H T G N L O
H A T X A N T Z K E R R X G L N T B N H V K
P T M D Z D N N K Q K V A V E F Z Z P A A
O W B N Z L L A W Z Q C O O T R L T K V Q N
S T Z N C C Y E M K X C T L S A K W N C D
T H V R M L H V R P P N C H T B G Z F M O C L
O V E N Y O J W L R A T E A M L R Q U R I
L E B W R L N S B H R O K V D I K I S M U N
E N P D G M R M T E S D Z C N J O B T E G K
I V I F Q L R L B N O L R C G G E A K T A N
G Y M V L H C W W G T B J E R F Y W R L Y
G C E Z D I F O B C P M Z A B S K K M M S V
E K R Q N X A K U M A I Q R X C L Y M T U
F W L X N R K R K R G M O M H T R D A T F A J
L E V O H S R C M E C T J T S G Q L B E J
M W B O L O I L Y T S L M C T I T W F M T
L P L G P O P W P O C K E T K N I F E D Z T T
```

127

P. 61 Types of Doctors

P. 71 Famous Inventors

P. 72 Things Invented That Change the World.

P. 77 Car Repairs

P. 92 Let's Play Ball!

P. 102 Find the types of scientist in the puzzle below.

P.119 So Many Jobs, Careers & Occupations A-L

P.105 People We Can Learn From

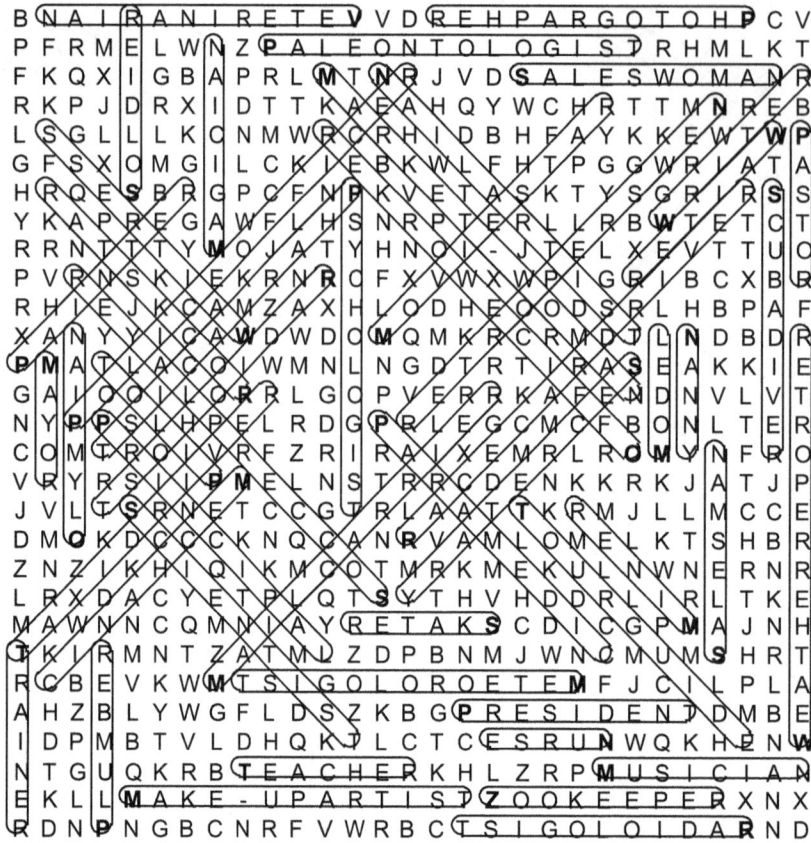

P. 121 Low Paying Jobs

P. 122 high Paying Jobs

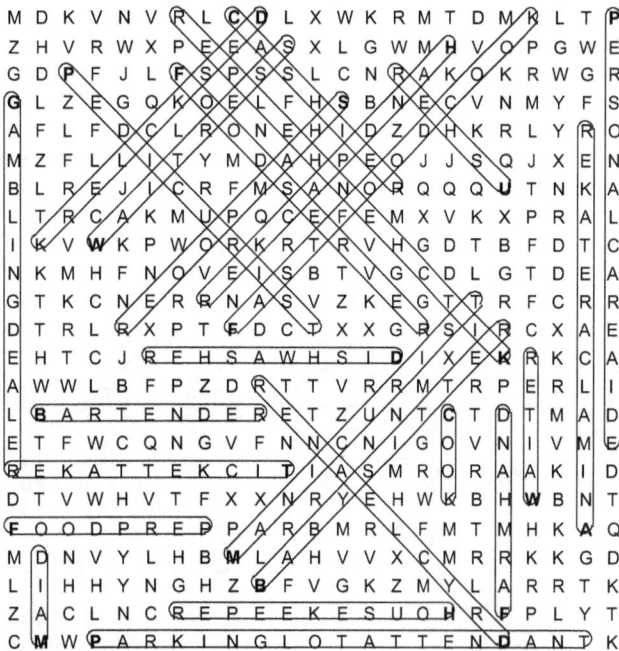

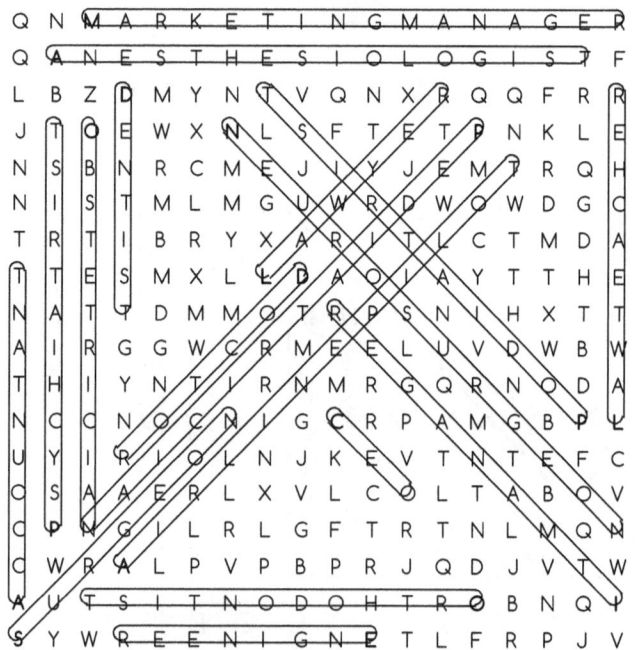

P. 118 Growth mindset vs. Fixed mindset Challenge

I like challenging myself because it helps me to gain new knowledge.

<u>Growth Mindset</u>   Fixed Mindset

If I make a mistake, I will not achieve my goal.

Growth Mindset   <u>Fixed Mindset</u>

The more I practice kicking, the better I will be at scoring goals.

<u>Growth Mindset</u>   Fixed Mindset

I tried to work this problem out, but I just can't get the right answer.

Growth Mindset   <u>Fixed Mindset</u>

I don't know what to write about because I'm not creative.

Growth Mindset   <u>Fixed Mindset</u>

If I set a goal, I can achieve it, even if it takes some time.

<u>Growth Mindset</u>   Fixed Mindset

My parents can't read well, so that's why I can't read well.

Growth Mindset   <u>Fixed Mindset</u>

In order to be successful, I must first experience failure.

<u>Growth Mindset</u>   Fixed Mindset

If I work hard and do my best, it doesn't matter if I win or lose.

<u>Growth Mindset</u>   Fixed Mindset

I will never be as smart as that kid.

Growth Mindset   <u>Fixed Mindset</u>

I don't understand fractions because I'm not good at math.

Growth Mindset   <u>Fixed Mindset</u>

I'm having trouble playing the drums, so I am going to switch to a new instrument.

Growth Mindset   <u>Fixed Mindset</u>

Thank you for choosing
Clever Children Gamebook

We hope you had a great experience with this book. We appreciate your support.

Please visit www.cleverchildrengamebook.villagetales.com to learn more about all our activity game books.

Join Our Mailing List

Be the first to know about new releases. Don't miss out on sales and important updates.

Leave Your Amazon Reviews

Show your support for Clever Children Gamebook and Sapo Children's Books, scroll to the reviews section, and click "Write a customer review."

Find Your Next Book On

www.childrens.villagetalespublishing.com

Ian & Applecat

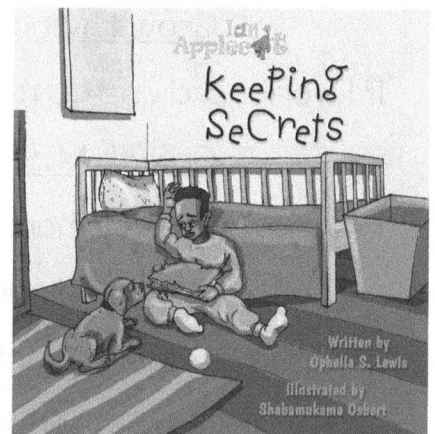

There's always something amusing in a preschooler's daily routine. Ian and Applecat is about a little boy who lives with his family in Monrovia. The series follows 4-year-old Ian and his puppy, Applecat, as he meets a number of milestones and acquires the ability to do things independently. Lucky for Ian, his eight-year-old sister, Lydia, is always there to help.

Adventures at Camp Pootie-Cho

One of the world's most diverse ecosystems sits in the middle of the Liberian rainforest —Sapo National Park. "Adventures at Camp Pootie-Cho" is a children's book series that shines light on the endangered environment and animals that live in this park. In the series, readers can learn about animals, the rainforest, and valuable life lessons. The stories feature fifteen animal campers and their fun experiences in the middle of the rainforest. Follow them on their journey. Visit website at www.camppootiecho.com. Meet the campers and staff.

Clever Children Gamebook

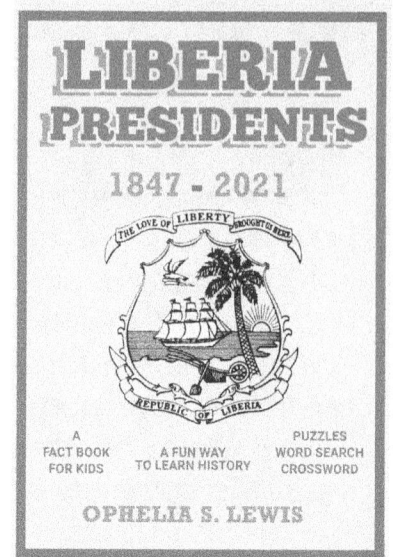

A Series of Children's Activity and Gamebooks

✓ Clever Children Gamebook provides children with fun learning, offering a variety of activities that build self-confidence, determination, and problem-solving skills through puzzles.

✓ Variety of activities: Puzzles, Word Search, Crossword, Mazes, scrambled letters that need to be unscrambled, secret messages to decipher, picture crosswords for young children, coloring pages, hidden pictures

✓ African and Multicultural puzzles

Benefits:

✓ Fun ways to help your child build basic skills – for kids ages 4-12

✓ Develops self-confidence: when a child solves challenging puzzles, imagine what that does for his/her confidence!

✓ Ideal for home or classroom use; entertaining and educational,

✓ Promotes attention to detail and increases vocabulary

✓ Hours of fun and entertainment to enjoy

✓ Perfect for rainy days, road trips, sleepovers, days off of school, lazy weekends, and more!

Reading Our World

Our world is filled with amazing people, places, and things; why not write books that will help teachers and parents include our world in our children's reading practice?

These books are notably playing a vital role in building a useful source of books African children can relate to culturally.

DRIVER ANTS ARMY

Written by Augustus Y. Voahn
Illustrated by Shabamukama Osbert

DRAMA on PIPE LINE ROAD

NEMEN M. KPAHN

Illustrations by
Shabamukama Osbert

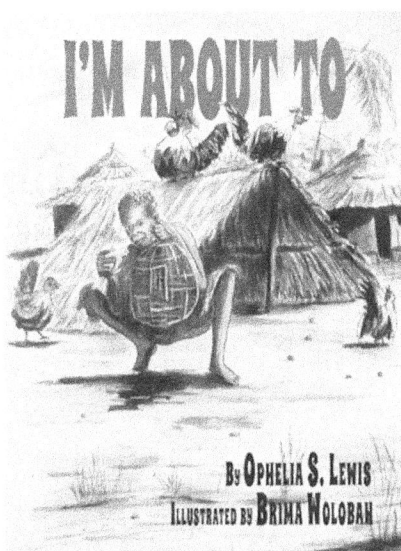

I'M ABOUT TO

By OPHELIA S. LEWIS
ILLUSTRATED BY BRIMA WOLOBAH

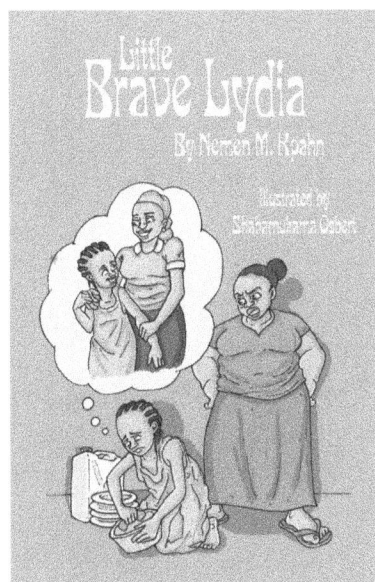

Little
Brave Lydia

By Nemen M. Kpahn

Illustrated by
Shabamukama Osbert

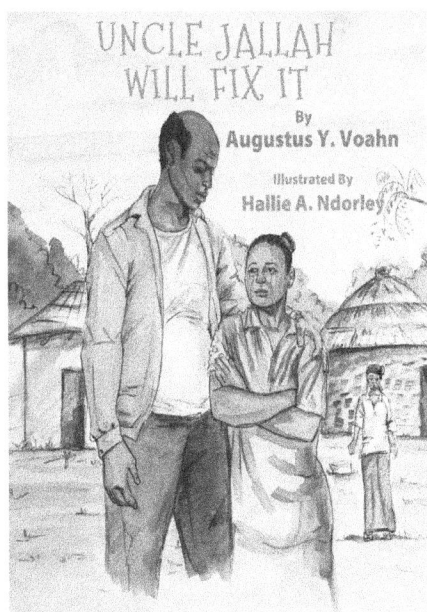

UNCLE JALLAH
WILL FIX IT

By
Augustus Y. Voahn

Illustrated By
Hallie A. Ndorley

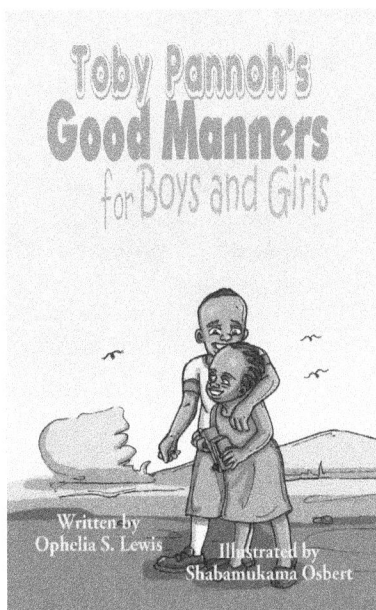

Toby Pannoh's
Good Manners
for Boys and Girls

Written by
Ophelia S. Lewis
Illustrated by
Shabamukama Osbert

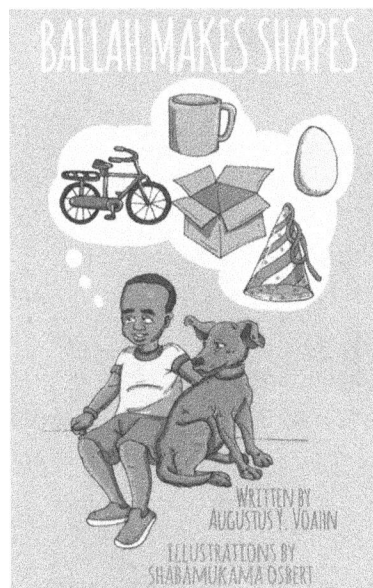

BALLAH MAKES SHAPES

WRITTEN BY
AUGUSTUS Y. VOAHN

ILLUSTRATIONS BY
SHABAMUKAMA OSBERT

Teacher Jeanette Kinder Kollege Workbooks

Teacher Jeanette Kinder Kollege Workbooks are designed to deliver the highest standard, and beyond, today's pre-elementary education. A strong start helps ensure a child is able to benefit from the learning opportunities available in today's kindergarten classrooms and homeschooling. These workbooks provide plenty of practice for children to succeed in kindergarten and beyond!

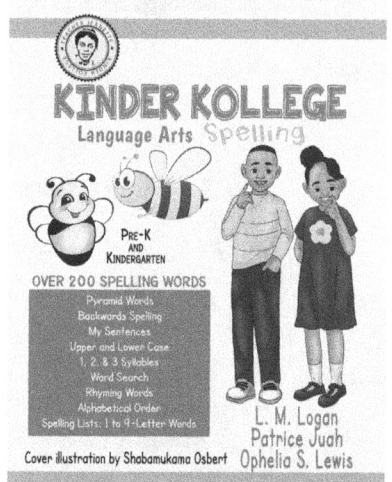

KINDER KOLLEGE
Language Arts Writing

PRIMARY WRITING
Learn to Letter
Writing Fundamentals
Primary Composition
Handwriting Pratice
Persuasive Writing
Accessing Information

L. M. Logan
Patrice Juah
Ophelia S. Lewis

Cover illustration by Shabamukama Osbert

KINDER KOLLEGE
Math
Primary Arithmetic

1
2
3
Pre-K and Kindergarten

Numbers & Operations
Counting 1-100
Measurement
Shapes
Data Analysis

L. M. Logan
Patrice Juah
Ophelia S. Lewis

Cover illustration by Shabamukama Osbert

KINDER KOLLEGE
Primary Bible Lessons

L. M. Logan
Patrice Juah
Ophelia S. Lewis

Cover illustration by Shabamukama Osbert

KINDER KOLLEGE
Primary Copybook

Handwriting Activities

Pre-K and Kindergarten

SUCCESS AT WRITING
Age appropriate line width
Bold lines for accurate letter placement
Lots of Activities & Coloring

L. M. Logan
Patrice Juah
Ophelia S. Lewis

Cover illustration by Shabamukama Osbert

KINDER KOLLEGE
Language Arts Reading

STRATEGIES & COMPREHENSION
Listening, Speaking, Viewing
Phonics and Fluency
Concepts About Print
Syllables in Spoken Words
Reading & Retelling Stories

Pre-K and Kindergarten

L. M. Logan
Patrice Juah
Ophelia S. Lewis

Cover illustration by Shabamukama Osbert

KINDER KOLLEGE
Language Arts Spelling

Pre-K AND KINDERGARTEN

OVER 200 SPELLING WORDS
Pyramid Words
Backwards Spelling
My Sentences
Upper and Lower Case
1, 2, & 3 Syllables
Word Search
Rhyming Words
Alphabetical Order
Spelling Lists: 1 to 9-Letter Words

L. M. Logan
Patrice Juah
Ophelia S. Lewis

Cover illustration by Shabamukama Osbert

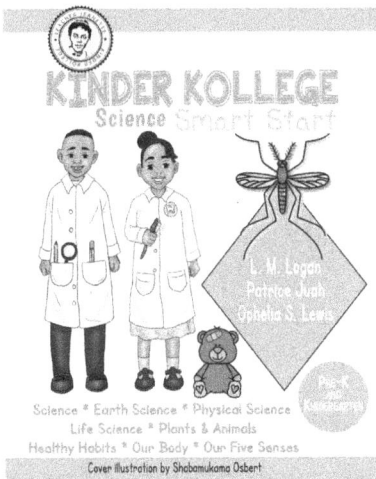

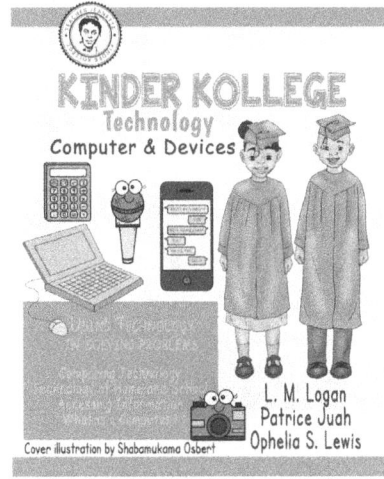

Learn more at our website
www.teacherjeanette.com

Available on Amazon & everywhere books are sold.

You Met Your GOAL!
Congratulations on Working Hard!
BE PROUD!

Awarded To:_____

For:_____

On the Date Of:_____

Signed:_____

Ophelia S. Lewis (Author)

Giving children a chance to learn is one of the most urgent priorities in Liberia. As a published author and humanitarian, Lewis takes on the dire yet fulfilling task of giving children an opportunity to start a solid educational journey. Quality education is key to any society's success; this ignites Lewis's passion for writing children's books.

Lewis began writing children's books in 2009. A mission to transform the limited books available with African characters in children's books today, drawing from her childhood for inspiration, she creates cultural-genre books with African characters all children can enjoy. Of her work, Lewis says, "The best way of getting people familiar with the importance of identity and own surroundings is through the eyes of childhood. Start at the earliest stage of life."

Lewis has created four children's book series: Reading Our World, Teacher Jeanette Kinder Kollege Workbook, Adventures at Camp Pootie-Cho, and Ian & Applecat. Joining the campaign to preserve Liberia's Sapo National Park in Sinoe County, Liberia, she created the series, Adventures at Camp Pootie-Cho, using native animals living in the park as characters people can easily fall in love with. Lewis is joined by other authors who write for the series. Learn more about her work at www.ophelialewis.com.

Shabamukama Osbert (Illustrator)

Shabamukama Osbert was born in the small village of Mbonwa, Ibanda District, Western Uganda. Art has always been a passion, even during his primary and secondary education. Mr. Osbert is a painter, structural designer, and illustrator. He loves art. During his free time, he enjoys photography, traveling, painting, and doing illustrations.

In 2016, he earned his bachelor's degree in industrial and fine art from Makerere University. Mr. Osbert currently lives in Kampala, Uganda.

Index

www.ingramcontent.com/pod-product-compliance
Lightning Source LLC
Chambersburg PA
CBHW081152090426

42736CB00017B/3285